AUTHOR

Since 2009, Chris Flaherty has written for the UK Armourer Magazine; Classic Arms & Militaria; and, Soldiers of the Queen Journal. He has advised major international museums on uniforms. For Partizan Press in 2014, he wrote and illustrated two books: 'Turkish Uniforms of the Crimean War: A Handbook of Uniforms'; and, 'The Ottoman Army in the First World War: A Handbook of Uniforms'. He co-authored and illustrated with Bruno Mugnai for Soldiershop Publishing: 2014 'Der Lange Turkenkrieg (1593-1606), Volume 1: The Long Turkish – War Habsburg Arrests the Ottoman Advance; and, in 2015 'Der Lange Turkenkrieg (1593- 1606), Volume 2: The Long Turkish War'. In 2015, he was a contributor (illustrator) to the Turkish Gallipoli Centenary Exhibition: 'From Depths to the Trenches: Gallipoli 1915', at the Isbank Museum in Istanbul. He was one of the contributors to, 'Philip Jowett, 2015 Armies of the Greek-Turkish War 1919–22', Men-at-Arms 50, Osprey Publishing. He authored a chapter on the, 'Ottoman Army in the Great Northern War' appearing in Stephen, L. Kling, Jr. (Editor) 2016 GNW Compendium: A Collection of Articles on the Great Northern War, 1700-1721 (Volume 2), The Historical Game Company. He has authored and illustrated for Partizan Press' Universal Wargames Rules Supplements: 'Napoleonic Small Siege, River Ship, Gunboat and Pontooning' (2016); 'Napoleonic Foraging, Insurrection, Marauders, Bakeries, Convoy and Encampment Wargaming' (2016); 'Napoleonic Balloon Warfare' (2017); 'Napoleonic Ottoman Army Wargaming Supplement' (2018); 'A Wargamer's Guide to WW1 Ottoman Army Uniforms' (2018); 'Napoleon's July 1798 Pyramid Campaign & the Egyptian Army' (2019); 'The Napoleonic Ottoman Army: Uniforms, Tactics and Organization' (2019). Since 2021 he has written and illustrated several titles for Soldiershop Publishing, including: 'The Sardinian Expeditionary Corps'.

PUBLISHER'S NOTES

None of unpublished images or text of our book may be reproduced in any format without the expressed written permission of Soldiershop.com when not indicate as marked with license creative commons 3.0 or 4.0. Soldiershop Publishing has made every reasonable effort to locate, contact and acknowledge rights holders and to correctly apply terms and conditions to Content. In the event that any Content infringes your rights or the rights of any third parties, or Content is not properly identified or acknowledged we would like to hear from you so we may make any necessary alterations. In this event contact: info@soldiershop.com. Our trademark: Soldiershop Publishing ©, The names of our series & brand: Museum book, Bookmoon, Soldiers&Weapons, Battlefield, War in colour, Historical Biographies, Darwin's view, Fabula, Altrastoria, Italia Storica Ebook, Witness To History, Soldiers, Weapons & Uniforms, Storia etc. are herein © by Soldiershop.com.

LICENSES COMMONS

This book may utilize part of material marked with license creative commons 3.0 or 4.0 (CC BY 4.0), (CC BY-ND 4.0), (CC BY-SA 4.0) or (CC0 1.0). Or derived from publication 70 years old or more and recolored from us. We give appropriate attribution credit and indicate if change were made in the acknowledgements field.
All our books utilize only fonts licensed under the SIL Open Font License or other free use license.

ISBN: 9791255892472   1st edition May 2025
S&W-057 - EGYPTIAN ARMY UNIFORMS 1830 TILL 1914
Written and illustrated by Chris Flaherty
Editor: Luca Cristini Editore, for the brand: Soldiershop. Cover & Art Design: Luca S. Cristini.

CHRIS FLAHERTY

EGYPTIAN ARMY UNIFORMS 1830 TILL 1914

SOLDIERS&WEAPONS 057

CONTENTS & INTRODUCTION

By the late 18th Century, the Mameluke Cavalry constituted the bulk of the Army of Egypt. Paid wages by the state, the Mameluke formed Regiments under their respective Bey. Each Mameluke-Bey, was also an Alay Bey: Regimental Commander, who led his own Regiment of Mameluke[1]. Traditionally, the Regular Army in Egypt was composed of seven Ojaqs, or Odjacklis: Militia Regiments, which had by 1797, some 18,000 enrolled men[2,3]. Included among the Ojaqs, was the Mustahfizan: Guards[4], an Imperial Janissary Regiment based in Cairo since the 16th Century[5,6,7]. The Regiment was also called the, "Guardians"[8]. The Cairo Mustahfizan was, "by far the largest of Egypt's Regiments, numbering several thousand by the end of the Eighteenth Century."[9] Following the Napoleonic Wars, Muhammad Ali, "saw European training, discipline, and tactics, as vital for improving his military power"[10]. The Egyptian Army divides into two main periods, before and after 1883 (when the new Egyptian Army was formally raised). Before 1883, there were nearly 20 Guard and Line Infantry Regiments having their beginning in the creation of the Nizam al-Jadid: New Organization[11]. Around 1832, there was the introduction of standard uniforms and equipment based on the European model. After 1883, the Egyptian Army was reorganized, and while it followed changes in the British Army over the same period, it still retained a distinctive appearance. The Egyptian Army between 1885 and 1914 saw introduction of the field service khaki uniform, in addition to its traditional summer and winter dress, which was relegated to Barracks wear.

CHAPTER 1: NIZAM AL-JADID ARMY (1830)..pag. 5

CHAPTER 2: NIZAM ARMY AFTER 1840..pag. 12

CHAPTER 3: NIZAM ARMY AFTER 1860..pag. 17

CHAPTER 4: MEXICO (1862 TILL 1867)..pag. 21

CHAPTER 5: NIZAM ARMY (1877 TILL 1883)..pag. 25

CHAPTER 6: KHEDIVAL GUARD..pag. 39

CHAPTER 7: INFANTRY AFTER 1883..pag. 48

CHAPTER 8: FIELD ARTILLERY..pag. 59

CHAPTER 9: BANNERS AND FLAGS...pag. 65

CHAPTER 10: RANK SYSTEM..pag. 70

REFERENCES..pag. 76

---

1 Ozturk, 2016.
2 Cole, 2008.
3 Ozturk, 2016.
4 Winter, 2003.
5 Walsh, 1803.
6 Fuccaro, 2016.
7 Ozturk, 2016.
8 Damurdashi, 1991.
9 Hathaway, 2002.
10 Dunn, 2021.
11 Dunn, 2021.

CHAPTER 1: NIZAM AL-JADID ARMY (1830)

In 1822, the first regular uniform given to the Fellahin Army,

> "were a mixture of French and Ottoman design motifs. Initially troops were outfitted in uniforms of French design, however, it was transitioned to a more distinct look as French elements were dropped from the overall plan. The men wore a coat over underclothing, they wore pants that ballooned between the hips and knees but were more traditional pants below the knees. The shoes were red felt and ended in an upturned point. The men wore red felt caps with almost no brim … The material from which the uniform was made changed from a type of soft material to broadcloth."[12]

The next set of regular uniforms given to the al-Nizam al-Jadid: the new regulation, used to designate Muhammad Ali's European-drilled forces[13]; was, "the first regular uniform issued to the Infantry recruited among the native Egyptians after 1832."[14] One set was for summer, and the other for winter. The summer uniform was a white linen jacket and Shawal: white baggy trousers – that became synonymous with the Egyptian Infantry. The 1832 winter uniform consisted of a low collared coloured jacket closed with upwards of fourteen pairs of small gilt metal ball-buttons, arranged closely to the closure seam on the front of the jacket. The buttons likely incorporated a loop system joining each pair to close the front of the jacket. Sleeves were close-fitting with a small open back seam. The jacket had plain buttoned shoulder straps attached. Under the collar a low black neck stock with a standing shirt collar was worn. Wide short pantaloons, were worn with tight-fitting leggings that covered the ankle (these items matched the jacket colour). These could also have been wide short knee-length bloomer pants worn with the same-coloured stockings. Red slipper shoes, or riding boots, "[were] … of red Morocco leather."[15] Some versions of the slipper shoes had heel counters, others did not, and commonly the slippers had long elaborately cut tongues. Cavalry Soldiers wore black riding boots with, "spurs of blackened iron, as in the French Army."[16] A wide green waist wrap completed the Soldiers' dress.

▼ An 1832 account of the Turkish Army, described details of the Egyptian uniform at the same time, gives the winter system of colour identifications[17]:

Generals and Senior Officers	Red jackets, trousers and leggings with heavy gold embroidery
Regimental Officers	Blue jackets, trousers and leggings with heavy gold embroidery
Junior Officers	Have a line of gold cord running down the front closure seam
Lifeguard Infantry	Red jackets, trousers and leggings
Line Infantry	Blue jackets, trousers and leggings
Cavalry	Blue jackets, trousers and leggings with Fez Badge
Artillery	Red jackets, trousers and leggings with Fez Badge
Surgeons	Light blue coat, with carmine cuffs
Field Apothecaries	Plain ash coloured coats
Cadets of the General Staff	Infantry Officers' uniform without badges and with different embroidery
Cavalry School Pupils	Wear scarlet Officers' uniforms

---

12   Bowden, 2016.
13   Dunn, 2013.
14   Bowden, 2016.
15   Knotel, 1969.
16   Knotel, 1969.
17   Knotel, 1969.

In 1832, "the Lifeguard Regiment … [was] … uniformed in red"[18]. While an 1832 account states: "[the] … Guard Infantry Regiment wears a chestnut brown uniform with more silk embroidery than the Line."[19] By 1833, the Nizam al-Jadid Army's Infantry consisted of three Guard and eight Regular Regiments[20]. The Regiments on paper had 4,000 Soldiers and Officers, "but rarely numbered more than 3,000 on campaign."[21]

Called the Greek cap, or the Tarboosh [Tarbuche, Tarboush, Tarbash, Tarbuch]: it was a low red strait sided Fez with dark blue or black tassels, and a flat top. Tarboosh appear to have had two lines of stitching visible around the base[22], which likely attached a stiffening cardboard lining to reinforce the sides and give its cylindrical shape. Crimean War Commentators noted, the Tarboosh could become quite unsightly after a good rain or two[23]. Cavalry Soldiers appear to have displayed a large brass badge on the front of the Tarboosh consisting of a crescent with crossed swords[24]. A crossed swords, under a six-point star, over a crescent version is also documented[25]. The Transport Troops Fez badge displayed crossed swords under a wheel over a crescent, and the Pioneer and Sapper's Fez badge was crossed axes under a six-point star over a crescent. Tarboosh were worn over a white skullcap - the Tequi, "a close-fitting cap, which is worn underneath it, with a part projecting down all around."[26]

OFFICERS

An 1832 account of the Turkish Army, which was actually describing the Egyptian uniform, states: "Generals' and other Officers' uniforms are mainly red, with gold embroidery varying according to rank."[27] Officers' jackets were distinguished with heavy gold arabesque decorations around the collars, seams and front displaying bars down the chest[28]. Lower grade Officers wore chest cords, while Junior Officers were distinguished with tape chest bars. Generals and Officers had heavy gold arabesque knots covering the entire sleave, from the cuffs to the shoulders. Massive gold arabesque knots were displayed on the pants crotch area, over the thighs, and over the knees. Additional gold arabesque decorations edged the pants pockets. Officer's wide waist wraps were striped green and yellow. A black or red waist belt (with gold tape edge) for the sword, with a circular clasp buckle, or snake clasp, completed the dress. Officers wore red riding boots with gold embroidery down the outer sides.

GREATCOAT AND OTHER EQUIPMENT

Soldiers wore a grey short single-breasted skirted greatcoat, with a low collar[29]. It was closed with six large gold metal buttons. The Officers wore a similar version with round cuffs, and it was more light

---

18	Bowden, 2016.
19	Knotel, 1969.
20	Dunn, 2013.
21	Bowden, 2016.
22	Norman, 1985.
23	Norman, 1985.
24	Cenni, 1906.
25	Charton, 1840.
26	Knotel, 1969.
27	Knotel, 1969.
28	Cenni, 1906.
29	Cenni, 1906.

grey-blue in colour[30]. The greatcoat was strapped around the sides and top of a plain black European styled square backpack. An 1851 illustration shows a small cylindrical valise with a grey cloth cover with closed ends secured with a drawstring revealing a red centre. The pack is brown with a white central closing strap running the full-length of the pack cover[31]. Soldiers wore white cross belts supporting a plain black European styled cartridge pouch, and hanger sword, in the case of the Junior Officers, or bayonet for Soldiers[32].

HORSE FURNITURE

The horse furniture consisted of a red bridle, incorporating a decorative red bridle hat, with yellow edges and corner tassels, and reins with rectangular brass open buckles[33]. Red horsehair pendants hung from the bridle, and from the horse's chest strap. The red or blue schabracke (depending on the uniform colour) was small and square ended with a wide tape border. The pistol tubes were brass, or leather, and the square covers were red or blue with wide tape borders. Officers had gilt tape borders, and the Soldiers used red ones. Even though spurs were worn, red enamelled brass Arab stirrups were used by Officers.

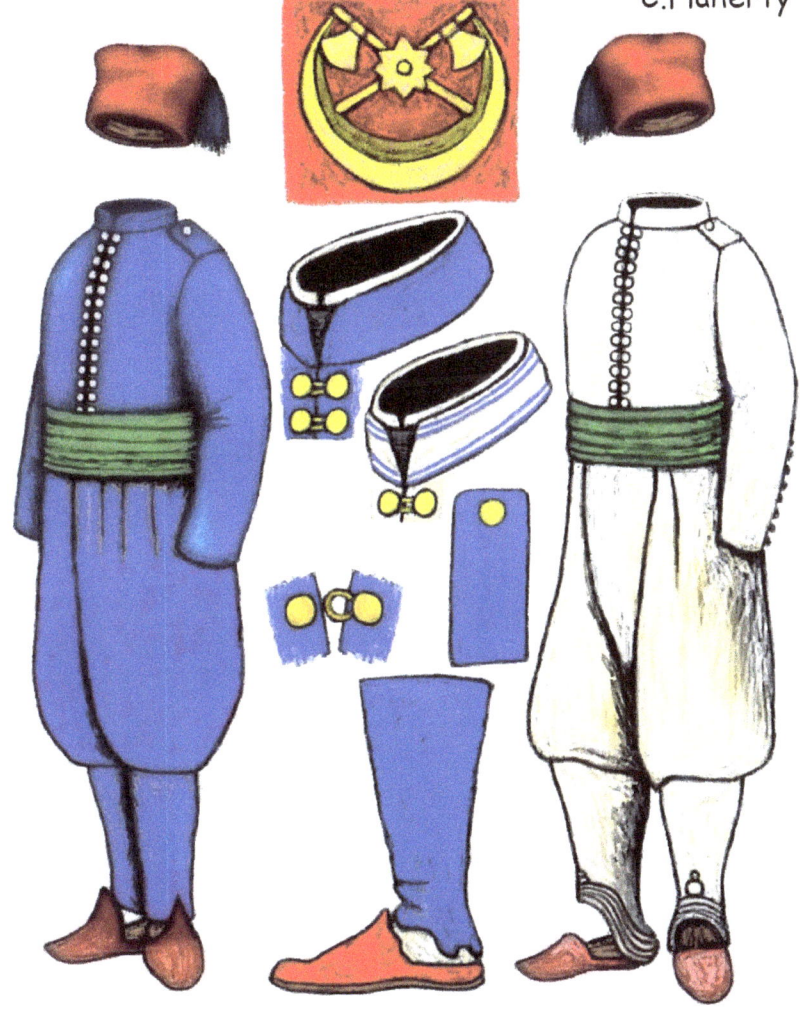

▶ Line Infantry Soldier showing collar, chest buttons, shoe and leggings details (1832). Pioneer and Sapper's Fez badge (1840). Infantry summer uniform and its collar details (1832).

30	Cenni, 1906.
31	Unknown, 1851.
32	Cenni, 1906.
33	Cenni, 1906.

▼ Mir-Lioua: General de Brigade (1832). Officer's blue saddle holster cover detail.

C.Flaherty

▼ Infantry Officer's belt, and possible buckle details. Infantry Officer wearing greatcoat (1832). Infantry Officer. Lifeguard Infantry Soldier. Junior Officer's jacket button details.

▼ Line Infantry Flag-Bachaouch: Sergeant-Major, wearing a greatcoat, with an Infantry Regiment's banner (1832). Line Infantry Sokolagassi: Adjudant Sous-Officier (1832). Line Infantry On-Bachi: Corporal (1832).

▼ Line Cavalry Soldier (1832), and Fez badge details from 1840, and earlier 1832 version.

CHAPTER 2: NIZAM ARMY AFTER 1840

Egyptian Soldiers after 1840 wore uniforms and insignia, which shared commonality with the new uniforms of the Turkish Army. A result of the 1841 Edict of Inheritance, that formalized the autonomous status of Egypt, as a privileged Province within the Empire, and secured hereditary succession to its Government for the family of Muhammad Ali, specified ways in which Turkish sovereignty should be symbolised, in particular with the Egyptian Army and Navy wearing uniforms and parading flags[34]. An 1848 watercolour painting of the Nizam: Regular Troops of the Turkish (Egyptian) Army on campaign[35]; and a mid-19th Century picture of an Egyptian Soldier at rest wearing an Ema'a: head wrapping shawl with long end tassels, wrapped around their Fez[36]; show a distinctive feature of the Egyptian Infantry shell jacket, that its front panels could be folded back. On summer uniforms these were unlined. The winter blue uniforms revealed red lining, and decorative white buttonholes, as can be seen in a later 1840s illustration of the Egyptian Infantry, misdescribed as, "Turkisches Militar"[37]. The unbuttoned jacket also revealed a red undervest. The pants are shown as light blue, and are either wide and tucked into black boots, or tighter-fitting with black shoes. The pants later changed to dark blue with broad red side stripes (as were worn in the Turkish Army at the time), and then later to loose-fitting dark blue pants, that could be plain or have side stripes. The white summer pants were broad and loose-fitting, and could have been short knee-length bloomer pants.

An illustration of an Egyptian Infantry Soldier leaning on their musket, circa 1830 to 1840[38], shows wearing a Tarboosh and white jacket with a low collar edged with double blue lines. An 1832 account states: "[the] … undress uniform of white linen … [is] … ornamented with blue lace."[39] The jacket is shown closed with a continuous row of small round buttons, and the sleeve seam from the elbow to the base of the cuff, has a similar continuous row of small round buttons – all features associated with the 1832 uniform. A wide red waist wrap, wide white pants and white leggings, that cover the ankles, end with four blue lines and decorative top knot. Red slippers complete the dress. By the 1850s, Chechias: a type of Fez, had come into general use. It was more rounded than the Turkish version. It was red bodied, and had long dark blue tassels. Chechias, like the earlier Tarboosh, were frequently worn over a Tequi: white skullcap that appeared as a white line under the brim of the hat. An 1854 photograph of Ismael [Isma'il] Pasha, said to be the Commander of Egyptian troops[40][41], shows an Egyptian Soldier wearing a long frockcoat – called the Litewka. The Litewka was also worn by the rest of the Turkish Army in the Crimean War era. The Litewka had come into use, during the Crimean War, as the Sultan had agreed, "to feed the … [Egyptian Soldiers] … and renew their clothing."[42] The Turkish Government also supplied Egyptian Soldiers, on their arrival in Constantinople with greatcoats, and cloth trousers, among other items[43]. An 1852 picture of Egyptian Soldiers showing all of them wearing Turkish Army greatcoats, and one of these displays a pre-1853 chest rosette indicating a Junior Officer in the Turkish Army[44]. The Egyptian Junior Officer wore

---

34	Peri, 2005.
35	d'Avennes, 1848.
36	Fahmy, 1997.
37	Unknown, 1840.
38	Unknown, 1840.
39	Knotel, 1969.
40	Fenton, 1855.
41	Fenton, 1855.
42	Slade, 1867.
43	Slade, 1867.
44	Preziosi, 1852.

chest bars. Crimean War Commentators describe Egyptian Infantry uniforms as sometimes a bit more elaborate than Turkish ones[45]. Further describing, they wore a dark blue jacket worn partially unhooked at the bottom, as these were fastened with hooks and eyes, rather than buttons. Egyptian shell jackets tended to be cut to pronounced pointed front ends at the bottom of the front vent. Describing the collar, cuffs and shoulder boards trimmed with red tape, as well as a very wide tape applied around the base of the collar. The Egyptian Army wearing older uniform styles, either reflected a preference for these, or that on arrival in Constantinople in their summer uniforms, they were supplied with older Turkish Army stocks, of winter uniforms by the Turkish Government. Photographs dated from 1855 show Egyptian Soldiers wearing dark blue or lighter grey trousers with red seam trim, tucked into short boots[46]. The Egyptian Soldiers are also described as wearing brown native slippers[47]. Crimean War Commentators also observed Egyptian Soldiers wearing long trousers shaded a somewhat lighter shade than the jacket, that was probably faded and without trim[48]. Various sources also indicate shoes (which could be civilian types) were commonly worn with white socks and tied with a single piece of lace.

OFFICERS' UNIFORMS

Officers by the 1840s are depicted in illustrations wearing plain blue frockcoats, with red collars, and red pointed cuffs, light blue trousers, black shoes, and a conical Fez displaying an oval brass metal shield[49]. The Fez shield may be a crescent and three stars badge, representing the arms of Muhammad Ali and his son Ibrahim (between 1820 and 1848). The Princely Khedival crown appeared in 1854. A painting showing Egyptian General - Selim Pasha at the Battle of Eupatoria (17 February 1855), depicts him wearing a plain blue frockcoat, with round cuffs and a low collar[50][51]. Rank was indicated by large gold fringed Russian epaulettes. An 1853 illustration titled: "grand review of Turkish troops by their Officers"[52], shows Egyptian Officers wearing long plain frockcoats. An 1860s era plain blue frockcoat with a low plain collar, closed by eight star and crescent buttons is displayed in a museum collection[53]. Silver French epaulettes with coiled fringes, and two double knotted lines ending with a diamond-shaped knot over plain blue pointed cuffs show the rank. An 1855 photograph of General Ismael Pasha, shows him wearing a fully embroidered court dress frockcoat, which could have been either Egyptian or Turkish in origin[54][55][56]. The round cuffs have tripointed flaps (with three large buttons) covered with gold floral embroidery. The trousers displayed wide gold side stripes.

CAVALRY

An 1840 account lists some fifteen Nizam: Regular Army Cavalry Regiments[57]. An 1854 description, of an Egyptian Lancer includes a blue and white French lance pennant to identify their Regiment[58].

45	Norman, 1985.
46	Fenton, 1855.
47	Norman, 1985.
48	Norman, 1985.
49	Unknown, 1830.
50	Hulland, 1857.
51	Williams, 1857.
52	Illustrated London News, 1853.
53	**National Military Museum.**
54	Fenton, 1855.
55	Fenton, 1855.
56	Fenton, 1855.
57	Charton, 1840.
58	Beamont, 1856.

An 1850s illustration shows an Egyptian Lancer Bimbachi: Major[59], wearing a green dolman with elaborate gold braiding, chest bars and buttons. A Fez, wide white pants, a wide gold waist band, and black riding boots completed the dress. The same 1850s illustration, shows a Lancer Soldier wearing a green shell jacket, with a green collar edged in yellow tape, and round yellow cuffs. Yellow tape runs down the front of the jacket and around its bottom edge. Several yellow tape chest bars with tasselled ends decorated the front of the jacket. The green horse shabrack is from the Napoleonic era, it had rounded front and pointed ends, with a broad yellow border.

PERSONAL EQUIPMENT

The 1832 Soldier was issued with a square plain black European styled backpack. The greatcoat was strapped around the sides and top of the pack using two side straps. Two looped straps hung from the base – the function of which are unknown. A tan-brown pack, with a small cylindrical valise is also depicted secured by three straps. The 1832 plain black European styled cartridge pouch was hung on a white cross belt. A white cross belt supported a bayonet, or Junior Officer's hanger sword that was either a D-Guard or a cross hilt. By the Crimean War Egyptian Infantry still used white cross belts[60]. Crimean War descriptions state commonly seeing a narrow belt circling the hips, however its function was unknown[61]. This feature, along with white cross belts are clearly visible in photographs[62], showing Egyptian (and not Turkish) Soldiers wearing what appears to be a standard belt under the shell jacket. A wide black waist belt, and a fife case on a wide black bandolier over the right shoulder was worn by the Musicians[63].

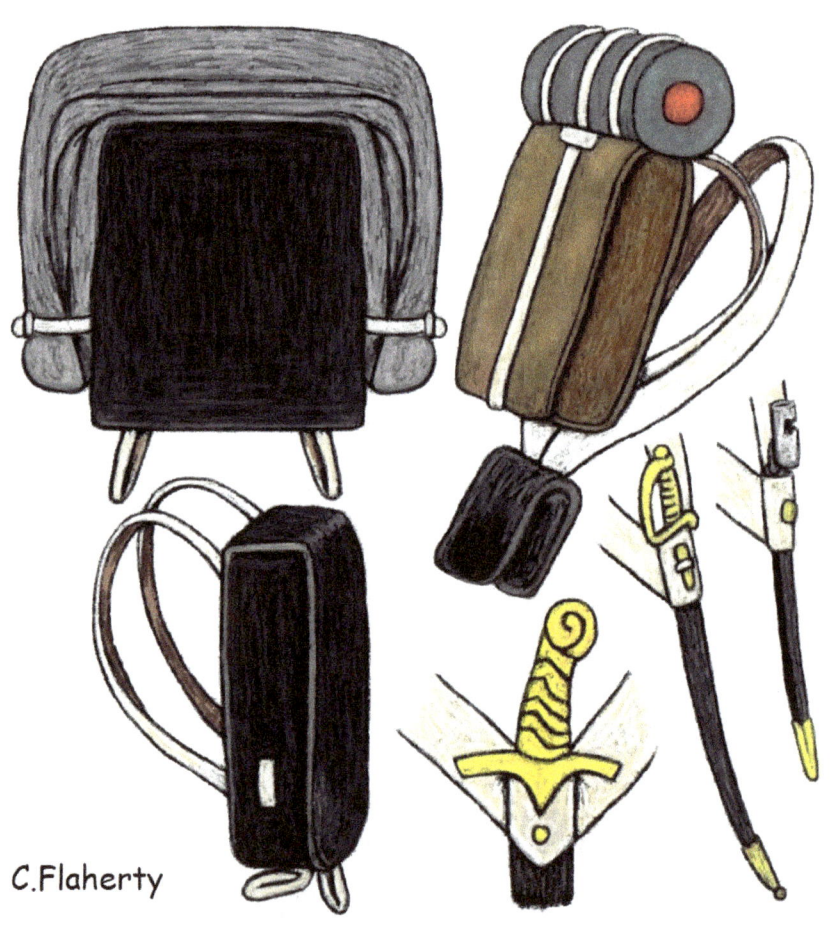

▶ 1832 Soldier's Equipment, bayonet, and Junior Officer's hangers.

C.Flaherty

---

59   Herwegen, 1850.
60   Norman, 1985.
61   Norman, 1985.
62   Fenton, 1855.
63   Norman, 1985.

▼ Soldier's white summer uniform (1848). General (1855). On-Bachi: Corporal wearing asymmetric chest bar (1840), and closed shell jacket.

C.Flaherty

▼ Infantry Officer (1848), with possible Fez shield details. Infantry Flag-Bachaouch: Sergeant-Major, wearing an opened shell jacket revealing its lining and decorative buttonholes in white tape, and holding an Infantry Regiment's banner (from 1848). Cavalry Soldier (1848). Lance pennant details, the colour combination representing each one of the different Regiments.

CHAPTER 3: NIZAM ARMY AFTER 1860

Coming back from the Crimean war the Infantry Soldier dated to 1860 is shown wearing a Turkish Army's Litewka[64]. It owed its influence on Prussian military purchases, over the 1840s, and the use of Prussian instructors. The Turkish Army's Litewka was generally loosely cut, had deep round cuffs with buttons along the rear seam slit. Depicted as plain blue, closed with several plain metal buttons, with a red collar and cuffs. Loose white pants, a low Fez with a yellow patterned cloth turban, and yellow slippers completes the dress.

An illustration of an Infantry Soldier from 1859[65], shows a white collarless shell jacket, closed by several large metal buttons, with round cuffs, which have a line of four small metal closure buttons running up the back of the seam, two above the cuff line, and two below it. A red and yellow cummerbund is worn over loose white pants tucked into short yellow leggings with grey ends. Black shoes with white spats and a low Fez completes the dress. Another, illustration said to be an Infantry Soldier from 1845 shows a nearly identical uniform, except the jacket has a low collar, a red waist wrap is worn under a narrow black belt with a rectangular brass buckle plate[66]. The other similarity is the short yellow leggings worn over the white spats have double black lines around the ankle ends.

An Infantry Officer dated 1859, is depicted in a summer uniform with a Regimental Award on their chest[67]. The Officer wears a white standing collar shirt, with a low black neck stock, with a white collarless shell jacket, closed by several large metal buttons, which has a line of several small metal closure buttons running up the back sleeve and cuff seam. A white waist band with red and blue patterns, is worn over loose white pants tucked into grey leggings with black decorations. Black shoes and a low Fez complete their dress. The red chest badge has a scalloped edge and is edged in gold. The badge appears to be embroidered with three words in Arabic script. Turkish Soldiers were often awarded in the 18th and early 19th Centuries with a Ferahi badge displaying text granting Soldiers the title of victorious or mighty.

▼ An unidentified mid-19th Century silver metal buckle based on British designs, incorporating a garter inscribed with Arabic script. The centre of the clasp displaying a star and crescent shield. The belt loops appear to have a lotus leaf design suggesting an Egyptian connection.

64	Unknown, 1860.
65	Unknown, 1859.
66	Goury, 1845.
67	Unknown, 1859.

CAVALRY

In 1863, two small Cavalry Regiments existed, and Khedive Isma'il planned to increase them to eight, but never fielded more than four[68]. These were divided between Lancers armed with bamboo lances, pistol and sabres, and Dragoons armed with carbines. A Cavalry Soldier dated 1859 is shown wearing a loose short plain grey, possibly light blue, jacket closed by several large metal buttons with a low red collar[69]. The plain round cuffs have a line of four small metal closure buttons running up the back of the seam, two above the cuff line, and two below it. Loose white pants are tucked into black riding boots with spurs, and a low Fez completes the dress. Another 1859 dated illustration of a Cairo Cavalry Officer, shows wearing a plain blue winter jacket with a hood closed by several large metal buttons[70]. Red round cuffs have a line of four small metal closure buttons running up the back of the seam, two above the cuff line, and two below it. Loose white pants are tucked into black riding boots.

▼ **Infantry Officer in summer uniform with Regimental Award on their chest (1859). Infantry Soldier in summer uniform. Infantry Soldier in winter uniform – Turkish Army's Litewka.**

---

68   Dunn, 2013.
69   Unknown, 1859.
70   Unknown, 1859.

▼ Cairo Cavalry Officer in winter uniform (1859).

▼ **Cavalry Soldier** (1859).

CHAPTER 4: MEXICO (1862 TILL 1867)

In 1862, Napoleon III requested a Regiment of Troops from Egypt, for the war in Mexico. Reduced to a Battalion of four Companies (446 Officers and Soldiers), and a Drogman: Interpreter[71]. Called the, "Ottoman Auxiliary Battalion"[72], the Egyptian Battalion was designated as the 19th Regiment of the Line, in the French Army[73]. The Battalion was also from the Egyptian Army's 19th Foot Regiment, as Mohamed Sa'id, Wali: Viceroy of Egypt. "acceded to this request, but sent only one Battalion from the Regiment of 19th Foot".[74] The Egyptian Battalion was allocated as an extra Battalion, "placed under the command of … the 3rd Zouave Regiment."[75] The Commanding Officer was a Bimbashi: Major, with a Yuzbachi: Captain as second in command[76]. Along with the Battalion, which arrived in Vera Cruz, a group of Impressed Recruits were described, "[as] … almost naked"[77]. Indentured by the Alexandrian Police, and were intended for use as Battalion Labourers. There were also 22 children (adolescence) from 10 to 15 years of age[78]. The presence of children was a common feature of North African armies, in both Tunisia and Egypt, as the Officers and Soldiers commonly owned boy servants, who were often dressed in military styled uniforms, and were armed themselves[79][80]. Two 1855 photographs show Egyptian Army Nubian servants[81][82]. One photographed is shown handing a Chibouque: Turkish Tobacco Pipe, and has been identified as, "a Nubian slave and a Copt pipe-bearer"[83]. The Nubian slave, appears to be a teenager, and wears a uniform, incorporating a short Tunisian-styled jacket, baggy breaches, white socks, and native slippers. He is armed with a long high-quality Turkish sabre. Another 1855 photograph shows two other Nubian servants wearing loose jackets over a shirt, short pantaloons, short boots, a broad sash round the waist, in which they carry a long dagger, and loose turban.

The Egyptian Soldiers' uniforms: "were well clothed, and equipped"[84]. Another account states, "[the] … smart uniforms gained immediate recognition when they landed at Vera Cruz."[85] In 1863, the French issued white cotton shirts locally found in Egypt, to maintain the Egyptian Battalion's original dress[86]. The shirts had a standing collar, and were closed with two buttons, with pleats down the front, while other versions only had, "simple stitching" [87]. The On-Bachi: Corporals are described wearing a white metal emblem on each side of the collar. A 1965 illustration shows an Egyptian Infantry Soldier wearing a French colonial service white fatigue overshirt with star and crescent collar badges[88]. Star and crescent badges were commonly used in the French Army to distinguish colonial Muslim troops. The illustration shows a red waist wrap. The 1965 illustrations are based closely on

---

71 Norman, 1992.
72 Ministry of the Armed Forces.
73 Hill, 1995.
74 Kirk, 1941.
75 Ministry of the Armed Forces.
76 Kirk, 1941.
77 Kirk, 1941.
78 Kirk, 1941.
79 Fenton, 1855.
80 Gernsheim, 1950.
81 Fenton, 1855.
82 Fenton, 1855.
83 Gernsheim, 1950.
84 Kirk, 1941.
85 Dunn, 2013.
86 Norman, 1992.
87 Norman, 1992.
88 Hefter, 1965.

an 1863 illustration of Egyptian Army Uniforms[89], but with some significant changes[90]. The Infantry Soldier in the 1965 illustration is shown with a short skirted white fatigue overshirt, while the 1863 illustration shows this garment with a long skirt falling well-below the wearer's knees. A special force of crack-troops from the Egyptian Battalion were, "distinguished by wearing a yellow brassard on the arm."[91] On 28 September, a new French military rank – that of Private 1st Class, for Soldiers of outstanding ability, was created. It was granted to many of the Egyptian Battalion's Soldiers. The number of special troops was not to exceed one-quarter of the total Battalion's strength.

It is said, on arrival in Vera Cruz, the Egyptian uniforms were put into store and replaced with, "uniforms based on those of the Tirailleurs Algeriens"[92][93]. The Tirailleurs Algeriens wore light blue Zouave styled uniforms; however, it appears the Egyptian Battalion received from the French Army in Vera Cruz, "[a] … red cloth monkey jacket"[94]. The 1863 French issue included a red Veste: jacket that were probably quite plain, fastening down the front with hooks and eyes, the bottom front cut to a slight point, possibly with some sort of trim or facings on the collar and cuffs[95]. In November 1864, the Egyptians are described, "[as] … clad in white uniforms, and turbans"[96]. In Mexico, the Egyptian Tarboosh were replaced by Zouave Chechias and turbans[97]. Later, a linen shell jacket was issued along with a blue necktie and shirt[98]. The shell jacket was described having seven white metal buttons down the front and round cuffs with two buttons[99].

The 1863 French issue included red waist sashes, and loose white cotton trousers or pantaloons, cinched below the knee with a draw-string, and worn with white linen laced gaiters and low black shoes[100]. The issue also had woollen overcoats with hoods, said to be of the Chasseur-a-Pied model – which was likely the Khedival Corps des Gardes version. A black waistbelt with a brass plate embossed with three stars and a crescent was issued in 1863, in Egypt. An 1884 illustration of Khedive Tewfik, shows this type of buckle[101]. Later belts with a snake clasp were issued by the French. It should be noted the snake clasp and belt also appears in the 1863 illustration[102], and it was part of the original 1832 uniform.

The 1965 illustration of one of the Egyptian Officers shows wearing star and crescent collar badges[103], on a shell jacket with 1832 era chest bars, and embroidery. However, an 1863 illustration of Egyptian Army Uniforms[104], shows a high collared jacket closed by a row of buttons, with a line of piping. Six lines of French knot and trefoil work cover the sleeve. Wide breaches, riding boots, and a wide waist wrap, and black belt with circular clasp completes the dress. The 1965 illustration shows a red belt with a silver metal buckle displaying Arabic script on the circular shield. The 1965 illustrations show the Egyptian captain in a summer light blue shell jacket, and the 1863 illustration shows much the same uniform consisting of a high collared jacket closed by a row of buttons, with a line of piping. A single line of French knot and trefoil work cover the sleeve. Wide breaches, leggings and European shoes complete the dress. Both the Soldier and the Officer are depicted in the

---

89	De Montaut, 1863.
90	Johnson, 1984.
91	Kirk, 1941.
92	Hill, 1995.
93	Service de Sante des Armees.
94	Hill, 1995.
95	Norman, 1992.
96	Kirk, 1941.
97	Norman, 1992.
98	Hill, 1995.
99	Norman, 1992.
100	Norman, 1992.
101	Loring, 1884.
102	De Montaut, 1863.
103	Hefter, 1965.
104	De Montaut, 1863.

1863 illustration wearing Turkish military Fez from the Crimean War era with a large metal button securing the tassels. An 1867 portrait photograph of Lieutenant Abd al-Rahman Musa - Capitaine au Bataillon Egyptien du Corps Expeditionnaire du Mexique[105], shows wearing a buttoned (showing seven small metal buttons) white jacket with narrow sleeves, and a small fall-down collar. A high white shirt collar, and small black bow tie appears above the closed collar. The sleeve cuffs have two gilt tape cuff chevrons. Wide white pantaloons are tied at the ankle with Turkish riding boots. A low Fez, and wide striped waist wrap, along with a waist belt for the sword, with a circular clasp buckle completes the dress. A 1935 illustration depicting the uniform shows the waist wrap was red and yellow striped[106].

▼ **French Army belt (with snake clasp), and Egyptian Battalion belt and buckle details (1863 issue). Infantry Soldier from the 19th Regiment of the Line (1867). Egyptian Battalion overcoat - Khedival Corps des Gardes version of the French Chasseur-a-Pied model (1863 issue).**

105 Choisy, 1867.
106 Boisselier, 1935.

▼ Egyptian Battalion Bimbachi: Major showing star and crescent collar badges (French Colonial Service), and Egyptian rank badge details (1862). Egyptian Battalion Officer's buckle. Egyptian Battalion Yuzbachi: Captain. Egyptian Battalion Soldier, wearing an Egyptian Infantry fatigue shirt, with a French yellow brassard - special force of crack-troops from the Egyptian Battalion, and collar details showing the French Colonial Service star and crescent badge.

CHAPTER 5: NIZAM ARMY (1877 TILL 1883)

Unlike the Turkish Army, the Zouave uniform was not adopted in the Egyptian Army, except for the Gendarmes, and later the Sudanese Battalions. The 1877 era tunic worn by Sudanese Infantry sent to fight in the Russo-Turkish War had a low rounded dark blue collar and pointed cuffs with white piping, and was closed by six buttons. Loose dark blue pants, with white piped seams, were tucked into long white gaiters with black shoes[107]. By 1883, the Egyptian Infantry tunic had a closer cut, with eight gilt buttons, and white piping down the front[108]. The high rounded collars were white, and pointed cuffs were dark blue (piped white). However, an old version Infantry tunic given to the Camel Corps, in 1885, had white pointed cuffs[109]. The Fez completed the dress. An 1883 dated illustration, shows the white summer dress in the field for Egyptian Infantry was a long collarless, loose long-sleeved white shirt, with calf-length pants, and local sandals completing the dress[110]. The low Fez had a quilted cover, and was wrapped with a turban made from a long cloth headwrap, that hung down the back of the neck. Identified as, "Arab Infantry", this shows a Soldier wearing an additional short open jacket, long trousers, with shoes and gaiters. A Sudanese Regular is depicted in an 1883 dated illustration wearing a plain low collared tunic with six buttons and trousers with shoes[111]. A low Fez is depicted, and narrow belt with a small plain rectangular buckle. The Soldier's greatcoat likely followed its 1832 pattern, including the Turkish Army version supplied during the Crimean War.

GENERAL AND STAFF OFFICERS

An 1870s illustration of a General shows wearing a dark blue tunic with gold floral embroidered chest, gold floral embroidered collar, pointed cuffs, which are topped by three gold cord chevrons[112]. A Fez, gold (with two or three red stripes) brocade belt with a square gilt metal crescent buckle plate, dark blue pants with wide gold side stripes and black shoes completes the dress. A Staff Officer is also shown wearing a single-breasted dark blue tunic, with red piping down the front, closed with nine gilt metal buttons. The collar has gold cord edging, followed by another gold cord insert (showing a wide dark blue line), and a line of gold floral embroidered around the base of the collar. The shoulder boards are blue with gold cord edging. Three lines of French knots and trefoils cover the sleeve length. The dark blue pointed cuffs have two back seam gilt metal closure buttons. A Fez, brocade belt, red pants with two gold side stripes and black shoes completes the dress.
A photograph of Thaddeus Phelps Mott, who was Aide-de-Camp to Khedive Isma'il, between 1863 to 1879, shows wearing a court frockcoat for a Pasha, with two lines of French knots and trefoils covering the sleeve[113]. The pointed cuffs are heavily embroidered with floral work around a crescent with three five-point stars. An 1884 illustration of Khedive Tewfik shows the same cuff badge[114]. A 1878 illustration of William Wing Loring, wearing a court frockcoat for a Pasha, has two lines of French knots and trefoils over cuffs heavily embroidered with floral work around a crescent with one eight-point star[115]. A Turkish Army Aides-de-Camp to the Sultan displayed a gold star, crescent, or a star and crescent badge above the cuff[116]. Three gold cuff stars and crescents represented the

---

107	Drury, 2012.
108	Unknown, 1883.
109	Unknown, 1885.
110	Graphic, 1883.
111	Graphic, 1883.
112	Unknown, 1870.
113	Leroux.
114	Loring, 1884.
115	Loring, 1884.
116	Askeri Muze, 1986.

Higher Military Supervisory Commission: The Office of the Khedive of Egypt, as Aides-de-Camp to the Turkish Sultan[117]. From the 1880s, a senior Turkish Officer was titled: Commissioner Extraordinary sent to Cairo, Egypt to represent the Sultan's sovereignty over Egypt[118].

▼ **William W. Loring as Pasha (1884)**[119]. A star and crescent badge have been worked into the floral cuff embroidery. The buckle plate has a crescent badge only.

---

117 Askeri Muze, 1986.
118 Peri, 2005.
119 Loring, 1884.

AMERICAN OFFICERS

A photograph of Raleigh E. Colston, an American Colonel in the Egyptian Army, 1873 to 1878, shows wearing a plain double-breasted frockcoat with large gilt star and crescent buttons, with heavy shoulder knots, and a low rounded collar[120]. The collar had a gilt cord running around the base, with a line of olive leaves running along the upper edge of the collar. A five-point star was displayed at the front of the collar on each side. A photograph of Alexander W. Reynolds, Egyptian Army Colonel, 1869 to 1876, shows a collar edged with two double gold cords, with heavy shoulder knots, and French aiguillette[121]. Two stars appear on either side of the collar front. The long double-breasted frockcoat cuffs were unusual, decorated with three vertical gilt tape buttonhole stripes, usually seen on doublet uniform cuffs (such as for the Royal Scots Fusiliers).

▶ Raleigh E. Colston wearing an Egyptian Army uniform in 1878.

OFFICERS' WINTER AND SUMMER UNIFORMS

An 1896 dated illustration of an Officer identified as Turkish[122], but more likely an Egyptian before 1883, is depicted wearing a plain dark blue double-breasted tunic, with gold epaulettes bridles, and six pairs of gilt buttons, with plain dark blue collar and pointed cuffs. Gold cuff chevrons form into trefoil ending with a diamond-shaped knot. Dark blue trousers with narrow red side stripes and black shoes complete the uniform. An 1882 illustration shows an Officer's uniform as a plain double-breasted tunic with a piped slanted front opening[123]. The collar is low, rounded, and open revealing the higher shirt collar. The cuff chevrons end with a trefoil diamond-shaped knot. A pre-1882 illustration shows an Infantry Officer wearing a dark blue double-breasted frockcoat piped red down the front, and around the skirt edge[124]. The low rounded collar is gold embroidered with leaves, gold tape covered shoulder boards, and dark blue pointed cuffs are topped with gold tape chevrons ending with a trefoil diamond-shaped knot. Dark blue trousers, black shoes, and Fez complete the dress. An 1882 illustration shows an Officer's summer dress uniform as a plain white high square fronted collared double-breasted jacket with slanted front opening[125]. The pants are either blue with a white side stripe, or plain white[126]. The rear vent of the jacket had two back waist buttons, and sideways opening pockets[127].

120	Anderson, 1878.
121	Fionillo, 1870.
122	Unknown, 1896.
123	Durand, 1882.
124	Unknown, 1883.
125	Durand, 1882.
126	Illustrated London News, 1882.
127	Illustrated London News, 1882.

OFFICERS' UNDERDRESS AND PATROL UNIFORMS

▲ **William Hicks Pasha and his Staff (1883).**

A photograph of Egyptian Army Officers in the Sudan, during the period of Hicks' Expedition, shows one wearing a dark blue tunic, with collar with wide gilt metallic tape around the outer edge[128]. The single-breasted tunic is close by a row of nine large metal buttons. A line of piping runs down the front of the tunic and around the bottom edge. The cuffs are pointed and topped with chevrons ending with a trefoil diamond-shaped knot. The Officer appears to be wearing large pear-shaped shoulder bords with a thick metallic tape edge. An 1883 photograph of William Hicks Pasha and his Staff[129], shows the Egyptian Officer's underdress uniform – a type of lighter weight, and simplified fatigue uniform for winter wear, as a loose-fitting short single-breasted jacket closed by six small metal ball buttons. The jacket either had a low rounded standing collar, or a small fall-down collar. The only decoration on the jacket was display of cuff rank chevrons ending with a lotus leaf knot. Small hip pockets with a rounded flap were positioned near the front of the jacket. The jacket also had small epaulette bridles. Dark blue pants, and black shoes completed the dress along with the Fez. A photograph of Egyptian Army Officers in the Sudan, during the period of Hicks' Expedition, shows them wearing in some cases the same light coloured underdress uniform[130]. One of the Officers wears shoulder straps, and the other narrow shoulder cords. The cuffs have chevrons topped with a trefoil diamond-shaped knot. The colour of the Officer's underdress jacket is open to question. An 1883 dated illustration shows Valentine Baker's uniform – which was also an under-

---

128　Sartorius, 1885.
129　Colborne, 1885.
130　Sartorius, 1885.

dress jacket, as light blue, including the breeches which have wide yellow side stripes[131]. A photograph of Egyptian Army Officers in the Sudan, during the period of Hicks' Expedition Force, shows wearing a dark blue loose-fitting fatigue jacket with five wide loose black tape bars down the chest[132]. The closure vent of the jacket is edged with the same wide black tape. The collar is low and rounded, and the pointed cuffs are topped with chevrons ending with a trefoil diamond-shaped knot. The Officer wears a pair of large shoulder cords. Another type of Egyptian Army Officers' fatigue jacket seen in 1883 was loose, with a low rounded collar. The jacket chest is decorated with several narrow tape bars, and the same narrow tape runs down the front. The cuffs are pointed and topped with chevrons formed into heavy metallic tape trefoil knots.

GENDARMES ZOUAVE UNIFORMS

Valentine Baker Pasha was largely responsible for developing the Egyptian Police, training them as a Gendarmerie, and military reserve, between 1882 and 1887[133]. An 1885 account, recalls, "the Mounted Gendarmes coming to station themselves are dressed in blue uniform with yellow facings, long boots, Tarbooshes, and mounted on grey horses"[134]. An 1883 dated illustration shows the Gendarmes wearing a light blue Zouave jacket, with a standing yellow collar, and yellow tape decorations[135]. The base of the cuff is edged with yellow tape, and a large yellow tape diamond runs up the back of the cuff, along the sleeve seam. Wide light blue pants with wide yellow side stripes are tucked into high white long gaiters with black shoes. Three yellow chevrons are displayed on the left upper sleeve.

An 1884 watercolour of a Sergeant of the 11th Sudanese Battalion[136], shows a collarless jacket with similar tape decorations, except three blue chevrons with yellow edges are displayed on both upper sleeves. Wide light blue pants with wide white side stripes (with blue lines) are tucked into dark blue puttees with black shoes. An 1896 dated illustration of Turkish Infantry[137], more likely show an Egyptian Gendarme, and this shows a collarless jacket with pointed cuffs that are edged along the top with yellow tape. Wide Light blue pants are tucked into high white gaiters with black shoes.

▶ The 1867 version of the Grand State Coat of Arms of the Khedivate of Egypt which features the crescent and three stars.

131	Unknown, 1883.
132	Sartorius, 1885.
133	Carr, 1901.
134	Sartorius, 1885.
135	Unknown, 1883.
136	Saumarez, 1884.
137	Unknown, 1896.

▼ An 1884 illustration of Khedive Tewfik[138], shows the same cuff badge as Thaddeus Phelps Mott, who was Aide-de-Camp to Khedive Isma'il. The buckle type with a crescent and three stars badge was also seen used by the Egyptian Battalion, sent to Mexico in 1863.

138   Loring, 1884.

▼ **Pasha Court (General-a-la-Suite Gala Dress) uniform (1877).** Pasha Court uniform's sleeve and cuff details with one star and crescent, and three stars and crescent (1877). Cuff details for the Higher Military Supervisory Commission: The Office of the Khedive of Egypt, as Aides-de-Camp to the Turkish Sultan (1876). Officer's sleeve knot and back of the cuff details. Zouave-styled Officer's frockcoat sleeve knot and back of the cuff button details.

▼ Colonel Raleigh Colston, collar and cuff details (1873 till 1878). Colonel Alexander Reynolds and collar details (1869 till 1876). Officer's French aiguillette details. Officer's brocade belt (two red stripes version) and crescent buckle details.

C.Flaherty

▼ Officer's brocade belt (three red stripes version). Infantry Bimbachi: Major's fatigue jacket with French sleeve knots and trefoil work, and gold cord edged shoulder straps (1883). Infantry Bimbachi: Major with cuff rank chevrons, with blue cuffs piped white (1883). Infantry Bimbachi: Major's British style patrol jacket with French sleeve knots and trefoil work, and shoulder cords (1883).

C.Flaherty

▼ **Mulazim-i-Evvel:** Full-Lieutenant (1877). **Bimbachi:** Major (1877). **Yuzbachi:** Captain wearing a lightweight summer uniform, and showing back details (1877).

▼ Staff Officer and shoulder board details (1877). Army Infantry Officer's white summer uniform, showing back details. Senior Officer's shoulder board details (1877). Collar details based on Khedive Tewfik's court dress frockcoat (1884).

▼ Sudanese Infantry Soldier (1877 Egyptian Contingent during the Russo-Turkish War), with an Infantry On-Bachi: Corporal's cuff chevron. Sokolagassi: Adjudant Sous-Officier's sleeve chevrons, Bachaouch: Sergeant-Major's chevrons, and Chaouch: Sergeant's chevrons details (1877). Infantry Soldier wearing a greatcoat (1877). Infantry Soldier with white pointed cuffs (1877). Possible shoulder board pattern.

▼ Gendarmes Regiment Bachaouch: Sergeant-Major (1883).

C.Flaherty

▼ Hicks Expedition Staff Officer (1883).

CHAPTER 6: KHEDIVAL GUARD

The Khedival Guard represented both foot as well as mounted Soldiers. Traditionally, a three-Squadron Regiment of Zirkhli: Cuirassiers served as a Bodyguard, from the 1830s. They were traditionally known in Egypt as the Zirkhagi: Iron Men[139]. The 1830s era armour consisted of a metal helmet with European chinscales and bosses[140]. It had a metal visor, and back protection resembling a 17th Century lobster-tailed pot helmet. It had a retractable arrow nose guard and crescent finial. The chainmail shirt had long sleeves, and was leather edged, and cut into large dragon's teeth. European gauntlets, a waist belt for the sword, with a circular clasp buckle, and strait bladed sword with a basket hilt are depicted. Black riding boots with spurs completed the dress.

CORPS DES GARDES

Use of a French Grenadier's bearskin can be seen in an 1863 illustration of Egyptian Army Uniforms[141]. Possibly depicting a Pioneer, as the axe, gauntlets, and apron are visible, as are the French epaulettes. The low collar shows a tape edge and a rectangular open buttonhole. The bearskin shows a plate on the front. A surviving Egyptian bearskin is clearly a French Grenadier's from the 1860s. Its semi-round sunburst front plate is modified with removal of the grenade badge adding a Horus badge. The catalogue entry from 1920, states:

> "6565.-Bearskin Cap of the Egyptian Corps des Gardes of Ishmail Pasha, whose uniform was similar to that of the French Imperial Guard of the 2nd Empire, and in which they were clothed at the opening of the Suez Canal. – Given by Captain H. Castle Smith, The Suffolk Regiment."[142]

Ishmail Pasha, otherwise known as Khedive Isma'il, Corps des Gardes bearskin appears to have been used around 17 November 1869. The particular Horus badge can also be seen in a painting associated with Mohamed Sa'id[143]. Another example of a large, stamped brass Egyptian bearskin semi-round sunburst plate is also known, and it displays a large star and crescent over a circular shield with an interlinked cursive 'SM' monogram, backed by three flags on either side displaying three stars and crescents. The use of French military costume reflected how:

> "[Mohamed] … Sa'id ordered extravagant uniforms, complete with solid silver epaulettes and buttons. Visually, he wanted his troops to be a-la-Francaise, and then some. French tailors and makers of military insignia sold vast quantities of material to the Wali, this despite the fact … in the case of heavy wool tunics and bearskin Grenadier … [caps, and] … helmets, were not ideally suited for use in a warm climate. Egypt's new Chasseur-a-Pied Battalions epitomized this trend. Although useful troops, whose training allowed them to be deployed as Skirmishers or Line Infantry, the desire to make them visual copies of their French counterparts entailed considerable expense. Sa'id authorized the purchase of 7,000 complete uniforms from Paris"[144].

From 1852, the tunic worn by the French Imperial Guard included several buttoned white chest bars with pointed ends. An Egyptian blue uniform from the 1860s era, is displayed in a museum collec-

---

139	Dunn, 2013.
140	Unknown, 1830.
141	De Montaut, 1863.
142	Royal United Services Institute for Defence and Security.
143	Delin, 1863.
144	Dunn, 2013.

tion, it has seven buttoned silver tape chest bars with pointed ends[145]. The collar and pointed cuffs are cherry red, and have wide silver metallic tape edging, that also appears along the coat skirts in a double line starting with the lowest chest bar. The trousers like the French Army at the time are cherry red with gold tape double side stripes. French silver epaulettes with coil fringes, and three lines of French knots and trefoil work up the sleave are used to show the Officer's rank for a Bimbachi: Major. Similarly, a later 1883 dated illustration of the Guardia del Ministra show them wearing a red frockcoat with gold chest bars with pointed ends, and pointed red cuffs with gold piping[146]. Blue pants with wide double yellow side stripes, Fez, and black shoes completed the dress. The Corps des Gardes Soldier would have been similarly dressed as the Officer, following the model of the 1852 French Imperial Guard's uniform. The side brush plume could have been white based on an illustration of the Khedival Mounted Lifeguard: Leibgarde 1. Escadron, in 1859[147]. The side cockade might have been green. An 1863 illustration shows the Bandmaster wore a French busby with a front plate (the details of which cannot be seen) with a white topped coloured plume and cummerbund[148].

KHEDIVAL MOUNTED LIFEGUARDS

The major change to the Zirkhli in the Mohamed Sa'id era was the loss of their cuirass and helmets, by the French maker: DELA CHAISSEE, and a return to sleeved hauberk: shirt of chainmail that covered the wearer down to their thighs[149]. Indo-Persian helmets with tall spikes and a camail that only left open the face, had a retractable nose guard with arrowpoints at either end. The cuirass with a new helmet, which had a similar appearance to the French 1852 Carabinier, was used to dress one of three Khedival Lifeguards Squadrons[150].

A Khedival Mounted Lifeguard identified as the: "Leibgarde 3. Escadron, Cario", is dressed like an Hussar, wearing a French busby with a yellow tape edged red bag and yellow cords[151]. The light blue dolman has a red collar, and pointed cuffs with yellow tape edging. The cords are yellow. The pelisse is red with black fur and yellow cords. A red cummerbund with a yellow mid-band, wide white pantaloons, and black French riding boots with spurs complete the dress. Another Hussar identified as a Guard, wears a Fez[152]. The light blue dolman has a light blue collar, and pointed cuffs with yellow tape edging. The cords are yellow. The pelisse is light blue with black fur and yellow cords. A white belt with a circular clasp buckle, light blue pants with a wide yellow side stripe, and black French riding shoes completes the dress.

Another Khedival Mounted Lifeguard identified as the: "Leibgarde 2. Escadron, Cario", is shown armed with a French wooden lance with a red over white pennant, and wearing a French-styled helmet of the Cuirassiers of the Imperial Guard, with a yellow metal semi-round sunburst plate[153]. Like the Guard Cuirassiers the helmet has a crest red tuft, and black horsehair. An 1863 illustration shows a white topped coloured side plume[154]. Shown wearing a light blue shell jacket with eight white (silver) tape chest bars with pointed ends, and silver metal buttons. The low collar is red. The pointed cuffs are light blue with a silver tape rank chevron. Silver French epaulettes with coiled fringes, and a red cummerbund with a silver mid-band, wide white pantaloons, and black French riding boots with spurs complete the dress.

---

145 National Military Museum.
146 Unknown, 1883.
147 Unknown, 1859.
148 De Montaut, 1863.
149 De Montaut, 1863.
150 De Montaut, 1863.
151 Unknown, 1859.
152 Unknown, 1859.
153 Unknown, 1859.
154 De Montaut, 1863.

A similarly uniformed Khedival Mounted Lifeguard identified as the: "Leibgarde 1. Escadron, Cario", wears a French Grenadier's bearskin without a front plate, and with a white brush plume and cords[155]. Shown wearing a light blue shell jacket with eight white (silver) tape chest bars with pointed ends, and silver metal buttons. The low collar is green. The pointed cuffs are light blue with green piping and a silver tape rank chevron. Silver French epaulettes with coiled fringes, and a green cummerbund with a silver mid-band, wide white pantaloons, and black French riding boots with spurs complete the dress.

An 1863 illustration shows the horse schabracke had a rounded front and long pointed back ends with a wide tape border[156]. A large cloth angled sideways facing star and crescent badge was added to the rear pointed ends. A cylindrical valise, or portemanteau: saddle case had a tape end ring, with a star and crescent badge in the inner circular patch.

▼ Bearskin Cap of the Egyptian Corps des Gardes[157].

155 Unknown, 1859.
156 De Montaut, 1863.
157 Royal United Services Institute for Defence and Security.

▼ Corps des Gardes Officer, Bandmaster, and Soldier (1859). Collar details for a Soldier.

▼ Corps des Gardes bearskin front plate version details. Zirkhli Bodyguard (from the 1830s). Khedival Mounted Lifeguard 2nd Squadron (1859). Zirkhli (1859), and buckle details (1863).

▼ Khedival Mounted Lifeguard 1st Squadron (1859).

▼ **Khedival Mounted Lifeguard 3rd Squadron (1859).**

▼ **Khedival Mounted Guard Hussar (1859).**

▼ Khedival Mounted Lifeguard (1863).

CHAPTER 7: INFANTRY AFTER 1883

Even after 1883, the Edict of Inheritance still remained in force, and the practice of wearing Turkish uniforms and parading flags continued under the British restructuring of the Egyptian Army. The Infantry winter tunic had plain white shoulder boards added[158], these were likely to have been dark blue with white piping previously. The back of the tunic displayed white piped vertical pockets with three buttons[159]. Red collar patches were added to the collar, and these had brass Ottoman-Turkish numerals distinguishing the new British trained Egyptian Infantry Battalions. The Sudanese Battalions wore numbered shoulder titles. The cuffs were now dark blue with a broad white tape chevron with two inner blue lines, which was topped with a white cord trefoil knot. Trousers were dark blue with broad white side stripes. Black shoes, with long white gaiters, and Fez completed the dress. Later blue puttees replaced the gaiters.

▼ **Ottoman-Turkish five (British made[160]) and three (Turkish made) numeral badges, for either the pre-First World War Turkish or Egyptian Armies.**

Display of Turkish orders such as the Osmani, established in 1862, were common in the Egyptian Army. Influenced by the British Army's 1879 Regulations, medal ribbons arranged along a bar, stitched directly onto the uniform or attached by a buckle mounted suspension bar, rather than hanging medals (often stored in little pockets sewn to the uniform), began to appear on ordinary Soldier's uniforms. Khedive Tewfik instituted the Khedive's Star in 1882. The Khedive's Sudan Medal was instituted by Khedive Abbas Hilmi II on 12 February 1897. Other metals such as the Egypt Medal were awarded for military actions involving the British Army and Royal Navy during the 1882 Anglo-Egyptian War, and in the Sudan (between 1882 and 1889), make an appearance on Egyptian Soldier's uniforms, including use of various clasps, like GEMAIZAH, 1888.

Over the 1890s, Fez used by the Egyptian Army, as well as by the Turkish Army got progressively taller and more conical. A variety of Fez covers were used, including the use of a Keffiyeh - cloth headwrap, placed over the head under the Fez, left loose, or wrapped around the base like a turban. This was commonly folded and tied around the Fez for storage with a cord[161]. A white cover (for the low Sudanese Fez that was worn initially) incorporated a back flap[162]. Headgear insignia consisted of coloured geometric shapes (worn on Fez covers-puggarees).

---

158   Army and Navy Gazette, 1900.
159   Union Postale Universelle Egypte.
160   Rod Wilson Collection.
161   Unknown, 1898.
162   Woodville, 1895.

BATTALION PUGGAREE INSIGNIA (1912)[163]:	
1st Egyptian Battalion	Green Dimond
2nd Egyptian Battalion	Maroon Rectangle
3rd Egyptian Battalion	White Dimond
4th Egyptian Battalion	Red and Green Rectangle
5th Egyptian Battalion	Blue Dimond
6th Egyptian Battalion	Violet Rectangle
7th Egyptian Battalion	Scarlet and Green Dimond
8th Egyptian Battalion	Yellow Triangle

In 1885, nine Egyptian Army Battalions, numbered sequentially, had been formed. In 1886, four new Battalions were raised. Later (in 1886), the 11th and 12th Egyptian Battalions were disbanded for reasons of economy. In 1891, there were a total of fourteen Infantry Battalions. In 1886, two new Sudanese Battalions were raised, and these were the 10th and 13th. In 1888, a Sudanese Battalion of Valentine Baker's Gendarmerie, was incorporated into the Army as the 11th Sudanese Battalion. The 11th originally wore light blue Zouave uniforms with yellow tape decorations[164]. In 1888, the 12th Sudanese Battalion was raised. In 1891, there were a total of six Sudanese Battalions: 9th to 13th. The following puggaree flashes, and plume hackie were used, for the Sudanese Infantry: 9th Battalion (green); 10th Battalion (black); 11th Battalion (red); 12th Battalion (yellow); 13th Battalion (dark blue); 14th Battalion (chestnut); and 15th Battalion (Maroon). British references state the Sudanese Infantry Band had a buff puggaree flash[165]. The Sudanese, were identified with a mix of Ottoman-Turkish numerals, as well as British pattern Roman numerals:

9th Sudanese Battalion	Green puggaree flash/hackie	Ottoman-Turkish 9 numeral
10th Sudanese Battalion	Black puggaree flash/hackie	Ottoman-Turkish 10 numeral
11th Sudanese Battalion	Red puggaree flash/hackie	Ottoman-Turkish 11 numeral
12th Sudanese Battalion	Yellow puggaree flash/hackie	Roman numeral XII
13th Sudanese Battalion	Dark Blue puggaree flash/hackie	Roman numeral XIII

The 9th Sudanese Battalion used an Ottoman-Turkish nine numeral. Whereas, the 1886 Cameron Highlander's presentation banner displayed an Ottoman-Turkish nine numeral in a shield on one side, and a Roman numeral IX in a shield on the other side. A surviving banner for the 10th Sudanese Battalion displays an Ottoman-Turkish ten numeral. Additionally, an 1889 painting of a, "Sergeant and two other ranks from the 10th Sudanese Battalion" clearly shows on the shoulder straps Ottoman-Turkish ten numerals[166]. In regards to the 11th Sudanese Battalion's insignia, this appears in photographs showing an Ottoman-Turkish eleven numeral displayed on its Fez puggaree flash, whereas the Battalion's drum features a Roman XI numeral[167]. Both the 12th and 13th Sudanese Battalions used Roman numerals[168]. The 12th Sudanese Battalion also displayed a scroll in Arabic under the Battalion badge with an Ottoman-Turkish twelve numeral[169]. The 15th Sudanese Battalion also used Roman numerals on their drum, as well as a scroll in Arabic under the Battalion badge with

---

163 General Staff, 1912.
164 Saumarez, 1884.
165 General Staff, 1912.
166 Donne, 1889.
167 Unknown, 1898.
168 General Staff, 1912.
169 National Army Museum.

an Ottoman-Turkish fifteen numeral[170]. In 1896, the Reserve Army, had its 15th, and 16th Battalions. In 1897, two more reserve battalions were raised: 17th and 18th Battalions. There is a collar tab, for the 16th Battalion, which has a green backed cloth square, set within the red collar tab, under an Ottoman-Turkish sixteen numeral. It is likely, this green patch indicated the Reserve Army[171]. A 1912 reference states: the 16th Egyptian Battalion was distinguished with a green and red square flash[172]. No examples of the Roman numerals badges have been seen, that could have been used by Sudanese troops; however, the British and Indian Armies regularly used title badges with Roman numerals.

▶ Example of the Crimean War period 20th Foot Regiment cap badge in Roman numerals.

▼ The 15th Sudanese Battalion drum displaying the Battalion badge with a Roman XV numeral, as well as a scroll in Arabic under the Battalion badge with an Ottoman-Turkish 15 numeral[173]. This says – Sudanese 15. The drum dates from around 1914 and has been given black hoops.

---

170   Armoury of St. James, 1914.
171   Private Collection.
172   General Staff, 1912.
173   Armoury of St. James, 1914.

TRANSITION TO THE FIELD SERVICE KHAKI UNIFORM

The Egyptian Army white summer wear uniform had seven front buttons, and two pairs of back vent buttons[174]. The pre-1883 version had dark blue piping along the top of the collar, and along the top of the pointed cuffs[175]. However, a 1976 illustration shows only red piping over the cuff with a loop at the point for an 1883 era Egyptian Soldier[176]. Sometime in 1885, the new khaki suit was introduced as a field service uniform relegating the blue and white uniforms to barracks duty[177]. Describing the Infantry Battalions' service uniform, which was also worn by the other arms:

> "[it] … was a brown jersey, sand coloured trousers and dark blue puttees. Head wear was the tarbush with a cover, the Egyptian Battalions having a neck flap in addition."[178]

The khaki suit was said to be darker, and not as yellow as the British Army version at this time, appearing as dark salmon sand coloured. The suit was loose-fitting, and the jacket was short-skirted, with six or five gilt-brass buttons down the front[179]. It had a low standing collar, and plain shoulder straps attached, with plain cuffs. Buttoned breast pockets were later added. The khaki pants were worn with blue puttees and brown shoes. The Fez was covered by a khaki cloth puggaree, and had a tie-on neck cloth. A dress version appears around 1899, that was used by the Sudanese Battalions which appears to have been a tall peakless stovepipe hat covered with khaki cloth, with a dark coloured top, displaying the flash and hackie on the right-side[180].

JUMPERS (BLUE AND BROWN KNITTED JERSEY)

A major change to the appearance of the Egyptian Soldier at the end of the 19th Century was the use of long wool knitted jumper, or jersey, rather than the traditional greatcoat. The first appearance in this era, was a long blue wool turtleneck jumper worn by the Sudanese, and was still in use around 1900 as the dress uniform version for winter[181]. Brown versions worn as part of the field service dress appeared around 1897[182]. Both the blue and brown versions were large enough to be worn over the jacket. The brown version was constructed of heavier wool, had an open collar neck (the jacket collar could be clearly seen), and had leather reinforced shoulder pieces to protect it from equipment load straps wear. Both the earlier, and later versions of the jumpers were long enough to cover the wearer's hips, and the equipment belt was worn over the jumper.

GENERAL STAFF

The Arkan Harb Riasseh el Geish: Headquarters Staff were distinguished with a black and white flash on their headgear, with a white and black plume hackie[183]. Worn on the British Officers' headgear, which in the field was an Egyptian Army pith helmet with a star and crescent badge. The Fez was worn on official occasions, without any badges or insignia.

174	Montbard, 1882.
175	Unknown, 1883.
176	Wilkinson-Latham, 1976.
177	Johnson, 1972.
178	Wilkinson-Latham, 1976.
179	Army and Navy Gazette, 1900.
180	G.K. 1899.
181	Army and Navy Gazette, 1900.
182	Wilkinson-Latham, 1976.
183	General Staff, 1912.

▶ Egyptian Army's General Staff tunic button. The general service tunic button displayed a star and crescent with a plain rim identical to the 1879 Turkish Army version.

OFFICERS' UNIFORMS

After 1883, the Officer wore one of three uniforms. Battalion Officers wore a higher quality version of the Soldier's tunic, with gold tape edging around the collar, and gold rank insignia. By the 1900s, Officers were commonly wearing an Egyptian version of the patrol jacket[184]. It had black braiding to the low standing collar and plastron front, with five horizontal rows of black cord frogging, decorated at the ends with black braid Austrian knots. The dark blue-black pointed cuffs were topped with gold cord chevrons worked into massive trefoil diamond-shaped knots, with the lower portions edged with flat black lace. Gold rank cords and Egyptian Army Officer's aiguillette were also used on this tunic type. The British Army Officer's patrol jacket was also worn (coming into use after 1896). It was a simple dark blue suit with four outside pockets, and low standing collar with Khedival crown collar badges. Rank shoulder boards were worn. Dark blue trousers, black shoes, and Fez completed the dress. The khaki suit introduced after 1885 for Officers had chest pockets, and was worn with the British Sam Browne and the pith helmet (for British Officers in the Egyptian Army).

▶ Infantry Piper, wearing summer dress uniform. Brugi: Bugler shoulder badge. Rombetgi: Drummer with long white gaiters, and shoulder badge details. Infantry shoulder board and tunic back details. Baltagi: Pioneer's crossed axes shoulder badge. Infantry Soldier's blue uniform wearing puttees.

---

184   Imperial War Museum.

▼ Infantry Officer's winter uniform, wearing the Egyptian Army Officer's aiguillette (after 1883). Officer's patrol jacket (British Army version), with British Sam Browne set, and collar details (after 1896). Officer's patrol jacket (Egyptian version), showing black cord frogging details, and wearing the Egyptian Army Officer's aiguillette.

C. Flaherty

▼ Infantry Soldier in white Summer dress with quilted Fez cover (before 1883). Egyptian Infantry (1883). Reserve Battalion Soldier's white dress uniform, with tall Fez (1897).

▼ Egyptian medal awards ribbon, directly attached to the tunic (with medals in pockets), and later ribbon bar for the Khedive's Star (1882), Khedive's Sudan Medal (1897), and Egypt Medal (1882 till 1889), with GEMAIZAH 1888 Clasp. Puggaree insignia for the 1st; 2nd; 3rd; 4th; 5th; 6th; 7th; and, 8th Egyptian Battalions (1912). Infantry Soldier, with tall Fez, and Keffiyeh, wearing summer dress (before 1885). Soldier's khaki suit (1885). 1st Egyptian Battalion Soldier wearing a brown service wool jumper (from 1897), and puggaree with Battalion insignia (1912).

▼ Arkan Harb Riasseh el Geish: Headquarters Staff headgear flash and plume hackie (1912). Pre-1914 collar gorget patch, for the khaki drill uniform, worn by General Officers and Staff Officers. General Staff Officer's khaki suit, with British pith helmet. Officer's white dress uniform wearing the Egyptian Army Officer's aiguillette. Officer's khaki suit with tall Fez. Standard service tunic button (based on the 1879 Turkish Army tunic button).

▼ Egyptian Battalions 1 to 18 collar patches, and shoulder boards for the Sudanese Battalions 9 to 13 (1885 till 1897). Collar details for the 17th Reserve Battalion (1897), 15th Reserve Battalion (1896), 18th Reserve Battalion (1897), and 16th Reserve Battalion (1896).

C.Flaherty

▼ 11th Sudanese Battalion white dress uniform, and puggaree flash (1897). Later era Sudanese stovepipe hat. 9th Sudanese Battalion puggaree flash (1890), and later 9th flash (1897). 10th Sudanese (1897). 12th Sudanese (1897). 13th Sudanese (1897). Sudanese in winter parade uniform with blue service wool jumper and Fez cover incorporating a back flap.

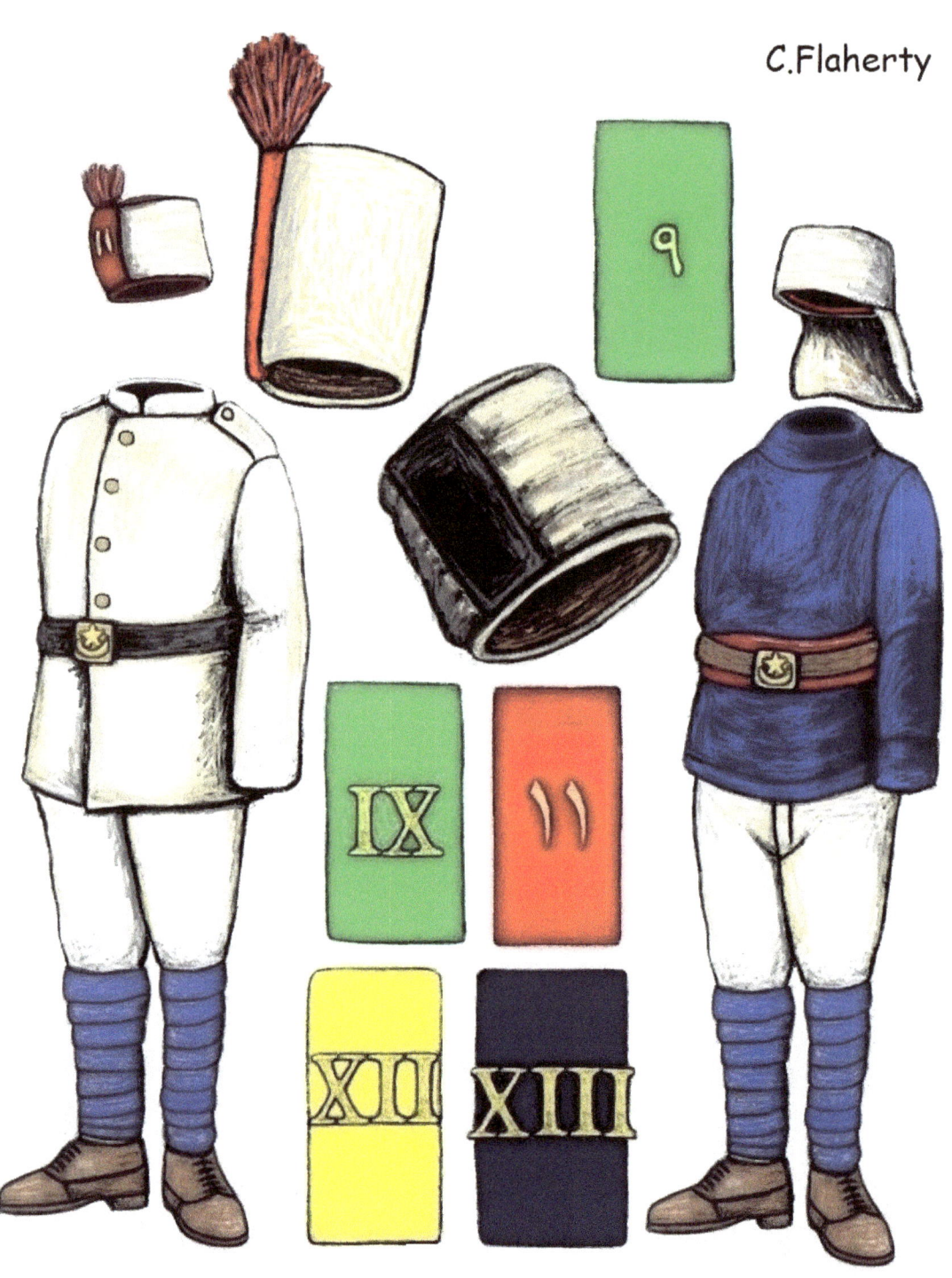

CHAPTER 8: FIELD ARTILLERY

The 1830s era Artillery wore red uniforms[185], and were distinguished with a Fez badge displaying crossed cannons under a six-point star over a crescent[186]. Crimean War Commentators describe the Egyptian Horse Artillerymen, and Foot Artillery wearing identical uniforms to that of the Army[187]. The only difference was the Horse Artillery Soldier carried a French Light Cavalry sabre (with a French patterned white leather knot), slung from a narrow white waist belt with a snake clasp. A plain white bandolier, was worn over the left shoulder and Western-type boots with attached spurs. The Egyptian Foot Artillery Soldier appear likely to have had red piping down the outer seam of their long dark blue trousers. They carried a large, Roman-type short sword in an elaborately cut and tooled frog on a white bandolier over the right shoulder (which suggested a Junior Officer). This may be referring to use of the British pattern 1848 Brunswick sword bayonet, which is clearly illustrated in an 1852 picture of Egyptian Soldiers[188]. According to Crimean War Commentators, the Foot Artillery displayed two different cuff types: two wide tapes circling the top of the cuff; or a wide tape circling the top with a narrow piping edging the bottom and rear opening. The significance is not known[189]. These are thought to represent Junior Officer's ranks.

An 1859 dated illustration of an Artillerie Unteroffizier: Artillery Junior Officer shows wearing a loose-fitting single-breasted dark blue long skirted tunic closed down the front with seven metal buttons[190]. This was the Turkish Army's Litewka. The round cuffs are dark blue with red edging, and a line of four small closure buttons run up the back of the seam, two above the line of piping, and two below it. Red trim runs around the base of the collar, and over the shoulder seams. A Fez, with dark blue trousers with red side stripes, and black shoes completes the dress.

ARTILLERY OFFICERS

An 1854 illustration showing a mounted Turkish Artillery Officer, in the Crimean War[191], is an Egyptian, who can easily be identified by his distinctive headgear: Tarboosh displaying a crossed-cannon badge. An 1880s illustration (likely pre-1883) of an Egyptian Horse Artillery Colonel[192], shows a long skirted blue single-breasted tunic closed with several gilt metal buttons, with red piping down the front. Red epaulette bridles, which could also be shoulder boards – as this was a common uniform feature around the 1870s, have gold edges. Five lines of French knots and trefoil work cover the sleeve. The pointed cuffs are blue, and have back seam gilt tape and a row of several small metal closure buttons – a feature of Zouave-styled Officer's frockcoats in the 1870s. The blue collar shows some type of badge, more likely Ottoman-Turkish script (however, it is not clear what this is); it could also be an Ottoman-Turkish script 'T' (ت). It is known this letter was used in the Turkish Army as part of its telegraph code adopted in 1909[193], for the word - Top-Askerlar: Artillery[194]. A Fez, and blue pants with wide red side stripes, and black shoes completes the dress. An Officer's brocade belt, and a gold cross belt supports a black Cavalry cartridge box.

185	Unknown, 1851.
186	Charton, 1840.
187	Norman, 1985.
188	Preziosi, 1852.
189	Norman, 1985.
190	Unknown, 1859.
191	L'Illustration, 1854.
192	Illustrated Sweet Caporal Tobacco Cards.
193	British General Staff, 1995.
194	War Office, 2008.

A 1991 description of an Artillery Officer's uniform on display in the National Military Museum (Cairo Citadel), likely from the 1870s era, stated:

> "the coat is a long dark blue model with maroon cuffs and a short standing collar edged in gold. The gold edging at the cuff consists of piping set in three equally spaced bands. The upper and lower bands swing up toward the elbow and form a 'V'. The middle band is fashioned into an inverted spade shape at the point of the 'V'. The pants are maroon with a wide dark blue stripe. A bushy blue tassel hangs from a maroon Fez. Leather accessories are black."[195]

The Artillery Officer's frockcoat on display, is closed with seven large gilt metal star and crescent buttons, with a dark red low collar, pointed cuffs and piping down the front[196]. The collar is edged with narrow gold metallic tape and the cuffs are topped with three chevrons terminating with a lotus leaf. This style of tunic stayed in use after 1883, and the only modification was shortening the skirt to stop in line with the base of the cuffs. The frockcoat has narrow gilt tape epaulette bridles that secure silver French epaulettes with coiled fringes. The Artillery Officer's star and crescent buttons are not the same as the version used by the Turkish Army's Artillery after 1876, which were a direct copy of the French Field Artillery crossed cannons and grenade button.

AFTER 1883

An 1883 dated illustration of an Artillery Soldier shows wearing a dark blue tunic closed with seven large brass metal buttons, with red piping down the front, and a low red collar and possibly dark blue shoulder boards with red piping[197]. Light blue trousers with red side stripes and black shoes complete the dress. After 1883, the Artillery wore a plain dark blue tunic with low red pointed cuffs, and collar displaying small brass grenades[198], which may have been the British Royal Artillery version, or Turkish Army's Artillery's grenade pattern based on the French version used at the time. Plain red shoulder boards displayed an Ottoman-Turkish script 'T' and the Battery number in Ottoman-Turkish numerals, for one to six[199]. Dark blue trousers with red piping, dark blue puttees and black shoes completed the dress.

▶ Egyptian Artillery tunic button based on the 1873 British Royal Artillery tunic button, displaying a breech loading field gun with shells, on terrain, under a star and crescent.

▼ A reconstruction of the likely appearance of the 1st to 6th Battery shoulder board details (after 1883).

C.Flaherty

---

195   Reinertsen, 1991.
196   National Military Museum.
197   Unknown, 1883.
198   Unknown, 1900.
199   Johnson, 1972.

▼ Artillery Officer's tunic (after 1883). Possible collar details including grenade badges. Star and crescent button, and Turkish Army's Field Artillery button (after 1876).

C.Flaherty

▼ Krupp field gun and Artillery Gunner (1890).

C.Flaherty

▼ Artillery Junior Officer (1859). Artillery Junior Officer (Crimean War). Artillery Soldier (1832).

▼ Egyptian Artillery Officer (1854). Fez badges for the Artillery and Transport Troops (1832).

▼ Horse Artillery Miralai: Colonel's shoulder board, sleave, and collar details (1877 till 1882). Artillery Soldier and possible shoulder board details (1883). Sleeve insignia details for an Artillery Bachaouch: Sergeant-Major, Chaouch: Sergeant, and, On-Bachi: Corporal (after 1883). Artillery Buluk Amin: Company Quartermaster Sergeant, with sleeve, and collar details showing British Royal Artillery grenade badges being used (after 1883).

CHAPTER 9: BANNERS AND FLAGS

Each Nizam al-Jadid Regiment carried a large square plain green standard, on a red flag pole with a gilt metal spear point[200]. The only decoration was a small red bow tied at the top of the pole with a gold fringe at the ends. An illustration of Egyptian Infantry, misdescribed as, "Turkisches Militar"[201], shows an Army Regiment's banner, of the later 1840s, as a green field with three gold crescents, which may have symbolised sovereignty over Upper and Lower Egypt, and Sudan[202]. It was also based on the personal flag for Muhammad Ali with the rank of Grand Admiral (Admiral of the Egyptian fleet), in the 1820s, with three crescents and stars on a red field[203].

▲ The first flag is for Muhammad Ali with the rank of Grand Admiral (Admiral of the Egyptian fleet), in the 1820s, followed by an Admiral of Egypt (crescent and three stars), followed by a Vice-Admiral (crescent and two stars), and Rear-Admiral (crescent and star).

Egyptian Army Regimental banners in the Crimean War period were likely the same as the rest of the Turkish Army, namely a red field with a silver crescent, as well as the star and crescent version. However, a green field with a yellow star and crescent was also possible. By 1883, the Regimental banner had a green field with a yellow star and crescent. Infantry Battalion banners after 1883, continued to use the green banner with a yellow star and crescent. The banners, "measure approximately thirty inches and appear square."[204] The main addition was a ribbon display above the star and crescent with the name of the unit without the use of a written numeral. Infantry, Cavalry

---

200   Cenni, 1906.
201   Unknown, 1830.
202   Reinertsen, 1991.
203   Unknown, 1841.
204   Reinertsen, 1991.

and Artillery Regiments were numbers sequentially[205]. In 1899, Egyptian Battalions began to apply battle honours from their previous campaigns. After 1899, banners had olive green fields with gold fringes, and the crescent and star were green with maroon edging. The Battalion's number was contained in a scroll above the crescent and star. All the scrolls were appliqued in red cloth trimmed with yellow, and the Arabic script was yellow. The 6th Battalion had a grey star and crescent, olive green fringe, and its Battalion name scroll was trimmed but contained no designation. The 10th Battalion had a grey-green star and crescent edged in red. The 11th Battalion's name was contained in a scroll above the star and crescent and a battle honour below it. The banner had a beige/grey repeated fringe. A 1991 list describing Battalion banners in the Egyptian Military Museum that were on display, identified the following details[206]:

BN.	COLOUR	BADGE	RIBBONS	FRINGE
9th	Green	Silver crescent and star edged red	Red with gold-yellow trim and inscription	Red/grey/grey repeated
10th	Green	Silver crescent and star without trim	Red with gold-yellow trim and inscription	Silver/red/red repeated
Infantry Rifles Battalion (1897)				
3rd	Olive	Gold crescent and star without trim	Red with gold trim and inscription	Gold
20th	Olive	Dark green crescent and star with red trim	Red with gold-yellow trim and inscription	Gold
Artillery	Blue Green	Gold crescent and star with red edging	Red without trim	Gold

▼ 1899 battle honours for each Battalion appeared either on the fly, hoist, or under the star and crescent badge:

BN.	FLY	HOIST	UNDER
3rd	5	5	NONE
4th	5	5	1
5th	1	1	NONE
6th	NONE	NONE	1
7th	3	3	NONE
9th	NONE	NONE	NONE
10th	NONE	NONE	1

▼ 1899 battle honours for each Battalion related to the following military events (list is not complete):

GEMEZEH (1888)	KHARTOUM - BATTLE OF OMDURMAN (1898)
TOSHKI (1889)	GEDID (1899)
ARGHIN (1889)	JEROK (1902)
FIRKET (1896)	BAHAR-ED-GHAZAL (1900 till 1902)
HAFIR (1896)	NYAM-NYAM (1905)
SUDAN (1897, then 1899)	TALODI (1905)
ABU HAMED (1897)	NYIMA (1908)
GEDAREF (1898)	KATFIA 1908)
THE ATBARA (1898)	

---

205 Toussoun, 1936.
206 Reinertsen, 1991.

▼ Flag Officer holding an Egyptian Government's flag (used after 1867). Regiment's banner (before 1883). Banner scroll detail. 12th Sudanese Battalion's drum scroll in Arabic.

The Egyptian Army's 10th Battalion banner is a green square, with a white fringe[207]. A large white Khedival crown (with red outlining), over a white Ottoman-Turkish ten numeral is displayed. Three red, and white embroidered ribbons are positioned around the Battalion number, for: TOSHKI, GEMEZEH (spelt – GEMAIZAH on the ribbon clasp, awarded for 1888), in two versions, one in Arabic, and then another in European script, and -ARGHIN-. The finial was either a crescent, or brass ornament in the shape of a Khedival crown. In 1886, the 9th Sudanese Battalion received a red banner from the Cameron Highlanders[208].

▼ **A reconstruction of the 9th Sudanese Battalion - Cameron Highlanders' presentation banner (1886). An Egyptian Battalion banner (from 1899 onwards). The 11th Sudanese Battalion's drum design (the possible early version).**

C.Flaherty

COMPANY FLAGS AFTER 1883

Each Battalion Company had a small rectangle coloured cloth flag, attached to a spear shaft, with a white Ottoman-Turkish numeral in the centre (giving the Company's number): 1st Company (blue); 2nd Company (black); 3rd Company (white); 4th Company (amber); 5th Company (green); and, 6th Company (vermilion).

---

207 National Army Museum.
208 Johnson, 1972.

▼ The 10th Battalion's banner showing details for awards: TOSHKI, GEMEZEH (in Arabic), GEMEZEH (in European script), and -ARGHIN-. The 1st to 6th Company Flags. The pole finial detail.

CHAPTER 10: RANK SYSTEM

The Egyptian ranks described here use phonic-based spellings, drawn from period accounts, as these likely retain original pronunciations. Many of the translation of these ranks are only known in French, which was the origin of this rank structure, influenced by the French in Egypt. A strong Turkish influence can also be seen in the naming. Alternative spellings appear in square brackets.

An 1853 illustration titled: "grand review of Turkish troops by their Officers"[209], more correctly shows Egyptian Officers displaying their breast rank badges, as these are known from Egyptian sources[210]. Crimean War Commentators observed how the Egyptian Infantry did not seem to have any visible rank insignia[211]. Unlike, the Turkish Army, the practice of using badge orders continued in Egypt, possibly as late as the early 1860s. An 1832 account of the Turkish Army, which was actually describing the Egyptian uniform, states:

> "The distinctions of rank are as follows: Lieutenant General ... [with a crescent] ... set with diamonds, with three stars, also set with diamonds, in the middle; Brigadier Generals wear similar crescents, but with only two stars. Lieutenant Colonels have a plain gold crescent with gold stars. Captains have silver stars; Senior and Junior Lieutenants wear plain silver crescents."[212]

The rank system initiated for the Nizam al-Jadid Officers from the 1830s, followed the 1820s flags used by the Admiral of Egypt, Vice-Admiral, and Rear-Admiral[213], turned into large metal badges for Generals, Senior and Regimental Officers[214][215]. Jewelled star and crescent chest badges (that could also be suspended from the collar, like a medal) identified a Mir-Mirdn: General de Division (three stars and crescent). As the most Senior Officer, in the Egyptian Army, he was also ranked as a Ferik: General de Division in the Turkish Army. The Mir-Lioua [Amir-Lewa]: General de Brigade, a Mir-El-Liwa [Liwa] in the Turkish Army, wore a jewelled two stars and crescent badge. A jewelled star and crescent badge identified a Miralai: Colonel. While a gold star, with jewelled centre, and gold crescent badge identified a Kaimakam: Lieutenant-Colonel. A gold star and crescent badge was worn by a Bimbachi: Major. A silver star and gold crescent badge for a Sakologassi: Adjutant-Major. A silver star and crescent badge for a Yuzbachi: Captain. A silver star and half-crescent badge for a Mulazim-i-Evvel: Full-Lieutenant. A silver star badge for a Mulazim-i-Sani: Lieutenant. A half-crescent badge for a Sokolagassi: Adjudant Sous-Officer.

JUNIOR OFFICER CHEST BARS

The rank system initiated for the Nizam al-Jadid Junior Officers was an arrangement of yellow chest tape bars and button tassels[216]. The 1832 version used a wide yellow tape bar across the chest coming to a point and tassel at each end[217]. By 1840, Junior Officers wore lace bars arranged asymmetrically across the chest, starting with a button, and tassel hanging from its ending[218]. Crimean War Com-

---

209   Illustrated London News, 1853.
210   Charton, 1840.
211   Norman, 1985.
212   Knotel, 1969.
213   Unknown, 1841.
214   Charton, 1840.
215   Cenni, 1906.
216   Charton, 1840.
217   Cenni, 1906.
218   Charton, 1840.

mentators noted an Egyptian Infantry Soldier, sketched at Varna, was seen with horizontal lines of tape down the breast, with tassels at both ends[219]. An 1850s illustration, titled: "Aegyptische Infanterie Oder Ehrenwache … [Egyptian Infantry]"[220], distinctly shows a figure with two prominent rosettes with tassels, displayed on one side of his jacket – this was an 1840s Turkish Army version of the Egyptian insignia for a Bachaouch: Sergeant-Major. Wearing Turkish, and not Egyptian insignia, was due to the fact, the Turkish Army was responsible for the supply of the Egyptian Army in the Crimean War.

▼ **Mir-Mirdn: General de Division wore a jewelled three stars and crescent collar or breast badge. Mir-Lioua [Amir-Lewa]: General de Brigade (jewelled two stars and crescent). Miralai: Colonel (jewelled star and crescent). Kaimakam: Lieutenant-Colonel (gold star, with jewelled centre, and gold crescent). Bimbachi: Major (gold star and crescent). Sakologassi: Adjutant-Major (silver star and gold crescent). Yuzbachi: Captain (silver star and crescent). Mulazim-i-Evvel: Full-Lieutenant (silver star and half-crescent). Mulazim-i-Sani: Lieutenant (silver star). Sokolagassi: Adjudant Sous-Officer (half-crescent). Bachaouch: Sergeant-Major with three chest bars from the 1840s era; Chaouch: Sergeant with two chest bars (1840s); On-Bachi: Corporal wearing a chest bar from the 1830s. Sabre-briquet frog displaying a multi-point star from the Crimean War period.**

C.Flaherty

JUNIOR OFFICER SABRE-BRIQUET

An 1855 photograph of Egyptian and not Turkish Soldiers[221], shows wearing a sabre-briquet on a black frog, displaying a multi-point star, attached to a white cross belt. This is a rank insignia mounted on the frog, rather than being worn by the Soldier. A large Roman-type short sword in an elaborately cut and tooled frog was also seen used by an Egyptian Foot Artillery Soldier by Crimean War Commentators[222], used to identify a Junior Officer.

---

219   Norman, 1985.
220   Herwegen, 1850.
221   Fenton, 1855.
222   Norman, 1985.

CUFF RANK CHEVRONS

Prior to 1883, Egyptian Officer's cuff chevrons either ended with a lotus leaf or trefoil diamond-shaped knot. The Saghkolaghsi: Adjutant-Major Battalion Staff had one simple cuff chevron. A Mulazim: Lieutenant, had a cuff chevron terminating with a lotus leaf knot. The Yuzbachi: Captain, showed two cuff chevrons terminating with a lotus leaf. A Bimbachi: Major, had three cuff chevrons terminating with a lotus leaf knot, and Miralai: Colonel wore three cuff chevrons terminating with a lotus leaf knot.

▼ Cuff chevrons for a Saghkolaghsi: Adjutant-Major Battalion Staff; Mulazim: Lieutenant; Yuzbachi: Captain; Bimbachi: Major (1877), and trefoil diamond-shaped knot details for a Bimbachi: Major (1883), and Miralai: Colonel's cuff chevrons (1877).

By the 1860s, a version of the pointed cuff chevron with double knotted lines ending with a diamond-shaped knot was in use. The 1870s saw widespread use of French knots and trefoil work covering the whole sleeve, at the same time as the system of cuff chevrons (with either the lotus leaf or trefoil diamond-shaped knot), which only covered the lower arm. The difference may be the result of where the uniforms were made, ordered from France, or made locally in Egypt. As a further mark of rank plain blue (or red for the Artillery) shoulder straps with gold cord edging were worn. Generals wore full gold versions. Heavy shoulder cords as well as French, or Russian-styled gold fringed or wire coiled epaulettes were also worn. The Khedive Tewfik displayed three stars on his epaulettes.

1877 ERA COLLAR STARS

Around 1877, collar stars are seen distinguishing various Officers, such as the Americans - Raleigh E. Colston, and Alexander W. Reynolds. It is possible, this was a short-term result of the American Officers adding insignia details according to their fancy.

AFTER 1883

After 1883, the system conformed to the British Army of the period using a combination of stars and crowns displayed on shoulder boards. A metal five-point star was used not unlike the Turkish Army Officer rank insignia (used after 1879), and a unique crown badge, known as the Khedival crown. This was a Western-styled crown with a crescent, or star and crescent at its top rather than a cross.

Gold (sometimes silver versions are known) shoulder cords displaying rank insignia are worn by Army Officers. The cords were combined with a special aiguillette, consisting of three cords slung across the chest connecting the shoulder cords together. A 1902 colourised photograph of a British Officer wearing their Egyptian Army uniform shows how the aiguillette cords were woven into the forward-facing edge at the shoulder end of the cord[223].

▼ **Gordon Pasha shoulder cords**[224]. Khedive Abbas Hilmi II's shoulder board rank insignia (after 1883). Egyptian Army Sirdar: General-in-Chief's shoulder cords (1905). After 1883, shoulder boards for a Sirdar (a); Ferik: Division Lieutenant-General (b); Lewa: Brigadier General (c); Miralai: Colonel (d); Kaimakam: Lieutenant-Colonel (e); Saghkolaghsi: Adjutant-Major Battalion Staff (f); Saghkolaghsi [Sakologassi]: Adjutant-Major (g); Yuzbachi: Captain (h); Mulazim Awal: Lieutenant (i); and, Mulazim Tani: Second Lieutenant (j).

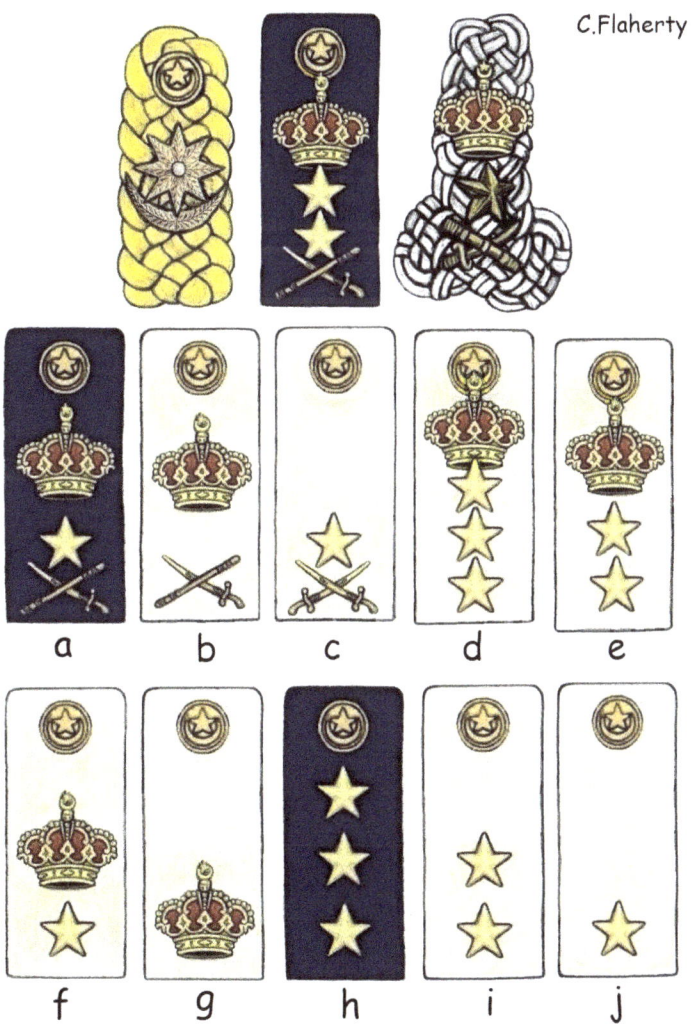

223   Lekegian, 1902.
224   Troedel, 1880.

JUNIOR OFFICERS: NON-COMMISSIONED OFFICERS' SLEEVE INSIGNIA (AFTER 1883)

By 1877, sleeve chevrons identified the Junior Officers. A set of three yellow upwards pointing chevrons on the upper arm identified an Sokolagassi: Adjudant Sous-Officier. A Bachaouch: Sergeant-Major wore three downwards pointing red upper sleeve chevrons. While a Chaouch: Sergeant wore two downwards pointing red upper sleeve chevrons. The On-Bachi: Corporal wore a red upwards pointing chevron over the cuff. After 1883, Non-Commissioned Officers' insignia were displayed on both arms. A system of white sleeve chevrons, with a blue inserted line along the lower edge, combined with a star, or Khedival crown, faced different direction and positioning on the upper or lower sleeve to identify the various ranks[225]:

Sol Talim	Battalion Sergeant-Major	Four reversed chevrons under a crown (lower arm)
Sol Tayin	Battalion Quartermaster Sergeant	Four reversed chevrons under a star (lower arm)
Bashshawish	Company Sergeant-Major	Four chevrons under a crown (upper arm)
Buluk Amin	Company Quartermaster Sergeant	Three chevrons under a star (upper arm)
Bachaouch	Sergeant-Major	Four chevrons (upper arm)
Chaouch [Shawish]	Sergeant	Three chevrons (upper arm)
Wekil-Shawish	Lance-Sergeant	Two chevrons (upper arm)
On-Bachi	Corporal	One chevron (upper arm)
Wekil-Onbashi	Lance-Corporal	
Baltagi	Pioneer	Brass metal crossed axes sleeve badge
Brugi	Bugler	Brass metal bugle sleeve badge
Rombetgi	Drummer	Brass metal drum sleeve badge
Serugi	Saddler	
Gazmagi	Shoemaker	
Nafar	Private	

▼ Post-1883 Non-Commissioned Officer's sleeve rank insignia: On-Bachi: Corporal (a); Wekil-Shawish: Lance-Sergeant (b); Chaouch: Sergeant (c); Bachaouch: Sergeant-Major (d); Buluk Amin: Company Quartermaster Sergeant (e); Sol Tayin: Battalion Quartermaster Sergeant (f); Bashshawish: Company Sergeant-Major (g); and, Sol Talim: Battalion Sergeant-Major (h).

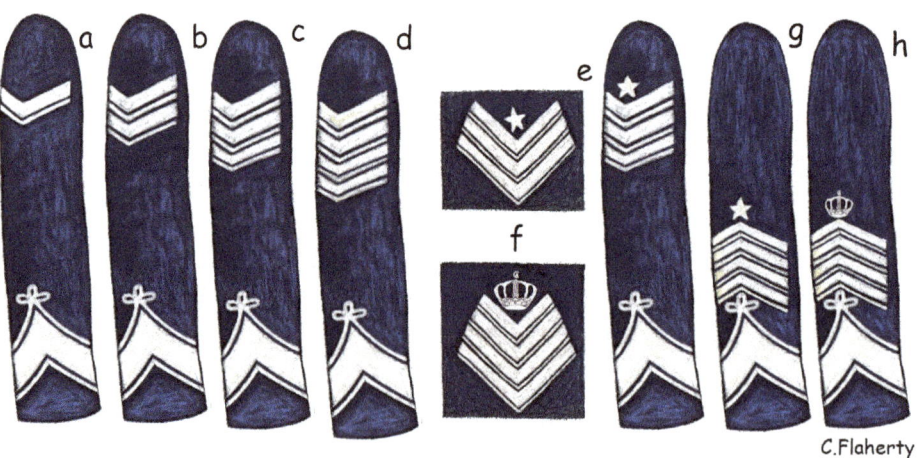

225 General Staff, 1912.

MILITARY SCHOOL CADETS (1902)

The Military School Cadets' winter uniform at the Training School (for Officer's sons), in Cairo, consisted of a plain dark blue tunic closed with seven large plain gilt metal buttons[226]. It had plain dark blue pointed cuffs, and its plain blue collar displayed a pair of plain white (which could also have been red) gorget patches with a small button. The shoulders displayed narrow dark blue double cords with a button near the collar. The same shoulder cords appeared on the white, and khaki jackets. Plain dark blue pants were worn with black shoes.

The Cadets' field order dress was similar to the Infantry Soldiers with khaki pants worn with blue puttees and shoes. A Fez completed the dress.

C.F

▼ The Egyptian Army's rectangular gilt metal star and crescent plate from around 1902.

C.F

226   Editor, 1902.

REFERENCES

- d'Avennes, P.E. 1848 Nizamior, Regular Troops of the Turkish Army at Kanka. Watercolour.
- Anderson, D.H. 1878 Portrait of Raleigh Edward Colston in Fez and Egyptian Uniform. Photograph. Richmond, Virginia.
- Armoury of St. James [The]. 1914 Sultanate of Egypt Period 15th Soudanese Infantry Side Drum.
- Army and Navy Gazette. Simkin, R. 1900 Types of the Egyptian Army. Illustration. Number 147 (3 March).
- Askeri Muze [National Army Military Museum, Istanbul]. 1986 Osmanli Askeri Teskilat ve Kiyafetleri [Ottoman Military Organization and Uniforms]: 1876-1908. Askeri Muze ve Kultur Sitesti Komutanligi Yayinlari.
- Boisselier, H. 1935 [-1952] Egyptian Battalion Officer and Soldier in Mexico, 1864-68. Unbound Folio, Paris, Cart.
- Bowden, J. 2016 The Armies of Egypt in the Years 1801-1832 (Part Two). History & Uniforms (May).
- British General Staff. 1995 [The] 1916 Handbook of the Imperial Army. Battery Press. Nashville.
- Carr, W. 1901 Baker, Valentine. Lee, A. Dictionary of National Biography. 1901 Supplement. London: Smith, Elder & Company.
- Cenni, Q. 1906 Egyptian Army Generals. Nizam al-Jadid Army Uniforms Circa 1830. Vinkhuijzen, H.J. [Collection]. New York Public Library [The]. Image ID: 1607016.
- Cenni, Q. 1906 Egyptian Army Mounted Infantry General and Regimental Standard. Nizam al-Jadid Army Uniforms Circa 1830. Vinkhuijzen, H.J. [Collection]. New York Public Library [The]. Image ID: 1607017.
- Cenni, Q. 1906 Egyptian Army Mounted Cavalry Officer, and Junior Officer. Nizam al-Jadid Army Uniforms Circa 1830. Vinkhuijzen, H.J. [Collection]. New York Public Library [The]. Image ID: 1607020.
- Cenni, Q. 1906 Egyptian Army Infantry Soldiers, Infantry Junior Officers, Summer and Greatcoat Dress. Nizam al-Jadid Army Uniforms Circa 1830. Vinkhuijzen, H.J. [Collection]. New York Public Library [The]. Image ID: 1607022.
- Cenni, Q. 1906 Egyptian Army Officer's Greatcoat. Nizam al-Jadid Army Uniforms Circa 1830. Vinkhuijzen, H.J. [Collection]. New York Public Library [The]. Image ID: 1607018.
- Cenni, Q. 1906 Egyptian Army Infantry Soldier. Nizam al-Jadid Army Uniforms Circa 1830. Vinkhuijzen, H.J. [Collection]. New York Public Library [The]. Image ID: 1607023.
- Charton, M.E. 1840 Forces Militaires de Mehemet-Ali. Uniformes et Insignnes des Differents Corps de l'Armee Egyptienne. Le Magasin Pittoresque. Paris.
- Choisy, E. 1867 Cabinet des Dessins, Estampes et Photographies: Capitaine au Bataillon Egyptien du Corps Expeditionnaire du Mexique. Photograph. Musee de l'Armee Collection. Reference: 993.121.73.
- Colborne, J. 1885 Hicks Pasha in the Soudan: Being an Account of The Senaar Campaign in 1883. London: Smith, Elder, & Company.
- Cole, J. 2008 Napoleon's Egypt, Invading the Middle East. Palgrave Macmillan: New York.
- De Montaut, H. 1863 Egyptian Army Uniforms. Illustration. L'Illustration, Journal Universel, Paris.

- Delin, H.P. 1863 Mohamed Sa'id. Painting.
- Damurdashi, A.D. Abd al-Wahhab, B.M. 1991 Al-Damurdashi's Chronicle of Egypt, 1688-1755 [Al-Durra Al-Musana Fi Akhbar Al-Kinana]. Brill.
- Donne, B.D.A. 1889 Sergeant and Two Other Ranks from The 10th Sudanese Battalion. Watercolour. National Army Museum Collection. National Accession Number: 1979-07-111-1.
- Drury, I. 2012 The Russo-Turkish War 1877. Osprey Publishing.
- Dunn, J.P. 2021 Genuine Diamonds or False Stones? Mercenary Loyalty in the Army of Muhammad Ali's Egypt. Studia Historica Gedanensia. Volume 12. Issue 1.
- Dunn, J.P. 2013 Khedive Ismail's Army. Routledge.
- Durand, S. 1882 Arabi Pasha and His Troops Ride Through Alexandria During the Anglo-Egyptian War. Illustration. The Graphic (22 July).
- Editor [The]. 1902 Egyptian Military Cadets: The Training School at Cairo. The Navy and Army Illustrated. Volume 15 (4 October).
- Fahmy, K. 1997 All the Pasha's Men: Mehmed Ali, His Army and the Making of Modern Egypt. American University in Cairo Press.
- Fenton, R. 1855 Ismail Pasha (Hungarian General Kmety) Ordering his Chibouque. Photograph. Library of Congress [The US]. Collection: LC-USZC4-9146.
- Fenton, R. 1855 Ismail Pasha (General Kmety) on Horseback, with Three Attendants. Photograph. Library of Congress [The US]. Collection: LC-USZC4-9232.
- Fenton, R. 1855 Nubian Servants and Horses. Photograph. Library of Congress [The US]. Collection: LC-USZC4-9233
- Fenton, R. 1855 Ismail Pasha (Hungarian General Kmety) and Mr. Thompson of the Commissariat. Photograph. Library of Congress [The US]. Collection: LC-USZC4-9156.
- Fionillo, L. 1870 Alexander W. Reynolds . Photograph. Alexandria.
- Fuccaro, N. 2016 Violence and the City in the Modern Middle East. Stanford University Press.
- G.K. 1899 Egypte – Soldats Soudanais. Publication Photograph.
- General Staff. 1912 Handbook of the Egyptian Army. London.
- Gernsheim, H. 1950 Roger Fenton: Photographer of the Crimean War. Chanticleer.
- Goury, J. 1845 Egyptian Infantryman. Picture. Anne S.K. Brown Military Collection: BDR 226200.
- Graphic [The]: An Illustrated Weekly Newspaper. 1883. Number 730. Volume XXVIII (Saturday, 24 November).
- Hathaway, J. 2002 The Politics of Households in Ottoman Egypt: The Rise of the Qazdaglis. Cambridge University Press.
- Hefter, J. 1965 Plate 263: Egyptian Battalion in Mexico, 1863-1867. Company of Military Historians. Volume XVII. Number 3 (Fall).
- Herwegen, P. 1850 Aegyptische Infanterie Oder Ehrenwache. Illustration. Anne S.K. Brown Military Collection: BDR 247581.
- Hill, R.L. Hogg. P.C. 1995 A Black Corps d'Elite: An Egyptian Sudanese Conscript Battalion with the French Army in Mexico, 1863-1867, and its Survivors in Subsequent African History. Michigan State University Press.
- Hulland, W. 1857 The Battle of Eupatoria During the Crimean War, 1855. Painting.

- Illustrated London News [The]. The Anglo-Egyptian War. Painting. Number 2256. Volume LXXXI (Saturday, 29 July).
- Illustrated London News [The]. 1853 Grand Review of Turkish Troops by Their Officers. Illustration with Pencilled Attribution of Army - Turkey, and 19 November.
- Illustrated Sweet Caporal Tobacco Cards. 1880 Col. Horse Artillery, Turkey.
- Imperial War Museum. Tunic, Service Dress: Sirdar, Egyptian Army (Kitchener). Collection Number: UNI 4023.
- Johnson, D. 1984 What Did the 19th Sudanese Really Wear in Mexico? Savage and Soldier Magazine. Volume XVI. Number 2 (April–June).
- Johnson, D. 1972 The Egyptian Army 1880-1900: Uniforms, Flags, and Numbers. Savage and Soldier Magazine. Volume VIII. Number 1.
- Kirk, R. 1941 The Sudanese in Mexico. Sudan Notes and Records. Volume 24.
- Knotel, H. Knotel, H.S.R. 1969 Uniforms of the World. London: Arms and Armour Press.
- L'Illustration [Journal Universel]. 1854 Turkish [Egyptian] Artillery Officer, Crimean War. Illustration. Number 593. Volume XXIV (8 July).
- Lekegian, G. 1902 Major-General Lord Kitchener of Khartoum. Coloured Photograph. Cairo.
- Leroux. Thaddeus Phelps Mott. Photograph. Vichy & Cannes.
- Loring, W.W. 1884 A Confederate Soldier in Egypt. Dodd, Mead & Company: New York.
- Ministry of the Armed Forces. The Ottoman Auxiliary Battalion. Chemins de Memoire.
- Montbard, G. 1882 The Crisis in Egypt: Types of Soldiers in the Egyptian Army. London Illustrated News. Number 2218. Volume IXXX. Saturday (3 June).
- National Army Museum [The]. Colour of the 10th Battalion, Sudanese Regiment, Egyptian Army, 1883. Collection National Accession Number: 1979-08-59-1.
- National Army Museum [The]. Side Drum shell, 12th Sudanese Battalion, Egyptian Army. Circa 1910. Collection National Accession Number: 1982-05-135-1.
- National Military Museum. Guard Officer's Uniform. Collection on Display. Cairo Citadel.
- National Military Museum. Officer's Frockcoat. Collection on Display. Cairo Citadel.
- National Military Museum. Artillery Officer's Frockcoat. Collection on Display. Cairo Citadel.
- Norman, C.A. 1992 The Egyptian Contingent: Mexico 1863-67. El Dorado. Volume V. Number 1.
- Norman, C.A. 1985 Turkish Uniforms of the Crimean Era. Soldiers of the Queen (Magazine of The Victorian Military Society). Issue Number 85.
- Ozturk, T. 2016 Egyptian Soldiers in Ottoman Campaigns from the Sixteenth to the Eighteenth Centuries. War in History. Volume 23. Number 1.
- Peri, O. 2005 Ottoman Symbolism in British-Occupied Egypt, 1882-1909. Middle Eastern Studies. Volume 41. Number 1 (January).
- Union Postale Universelle Egypte. Egyptian Quarters at Abbassiez. Photograph 7658. Cairo (Egypt).
- Preziosi, A [Count]. 1852 [-1857] Egyptian Soldiers of the Ottoman Army. Watercolour.
- Reinertsen, R.R. 1991 Egyptian Military Museum: Uniform and Flag Notes. The Courier. Volume IX. Number 6.

- Royal United Services Institute for Defence and Security. Egyptian Bearskin Cap. Museum Collection. Item Number 6565.
- Sartorius, E.I. 1885 Three Months in the Soudan. London: Kegan Paul, Trench & Company.
- Saumarez, G.leM. 1884 A Sergeant of XI Sudanese. Painting. Anne S.K. Brown Military Collection Item BDR: 8gy2p2fs.
- Service de Sante des Armees [Archives Historiques]. Tailor's Designs of a Uniform and Equipment for the Egyptian Sudanese Battalion. Colour Sketches by Doctor Fuzier, French Medical Corps. Les Collections du Musee du Service de Sante des Armees. Val-de-Grace, Paris.
- Slade, A. 1867 Turkey and the Crimean War: A Narrative of Historical Events. London: Smith, Elder and Co.
- Toussoun, O. [Prince]. 1936 [Mahmoud Sabit, Translator, 2019] al-Jaysh al-Misri fi al-Harb al-Rusiyah al-Ma'Rufah bi-Harb al-Qirm, 1853-1855 [The Egyptian Army in the War in Russia: Known as the War in the Crimea]. Cairo.
- Troedel. 1880 Major General Charles George Gordon (Late Governor General of Sudan). Colour Lithograph. Troedel & Company, Melbourne. The Australian War Memorial. Accession Number: ART50014.
- Unknown. 1900 Egypt – Non-Com. Officer. Artillery. Cigarette Card Illustration. Vinkhuijzen, H.J. [Collection]. New York Public Library [The]. Image ID: 1607015.
- Unknown. 1898 [-1900] Spielleute der Sudanesen-Infanterie. Colourized Publication Photograph. Vinkhuijzen, H.J. [Collection]. New York Public Library [The]. Image ID: 1607007.
- Unknown. 1898 [-1900] Gruppe der Anglo-Agyptisehen Infanterie. Colourized Publication Photograph. Vinkhuijzen, H.J. [Collection]. New York Public Library [The]. Image ID: 1607006.
- Unknown. 1896 [-1909] Turkey - Infantry of the Line, Private and Officer, Review Order. Vinkhuijzen, H.J. [Collection]. New York Public Library [The]. Image ID: 435730.
- Unknown. 1885 [1898-1820]. Kameelcorps der Egyptischen Armee. Vinkhuijzen, H.J. [Collection]. New York Public Library [The]. Image ID: 1607008.
- Unknown. 1883 [1898-1820] Egyptian Army – Various Types. Vinkhuijzen, H.J. [Collection]. New York Public Library [The]. Image ID: 1607001.
- Unknown. 1870 Egyptian General. Vinkhuijzen, H.J. [Collection]. New York Public Library [The]. Image ID: 1607000.
- Unknown. 1860 Egyptian Infantry Soldier in Blue Litewka. Vinkhuijzen, H.J. [Collection]. New York Public Library [The]. Image ID: 1606992.
- Unknown. 1859 Egyptian Infantry Officer With Chest Badge. Vinkhuijzen, H.J. [Collection]. New York Public Library [The]. Image ID: 1606994.
- Unknown. 1859 Cairo Cavalry Officer Wearing Winter Jacket. Vinkhuijzen, H.J. [Collection]. New York Public Library [The]. Image ID: 1606989.
- Unknown. 1859 Egyptian Cavalry Soldier. Vinkhuijzen, H.J. [Collection]. New York Public Library [The]. Image ID: 1606990.
- Unknown. 1859 Egyptian Infantry Soldier in Summer White Uniform. Vinkhuijzen, H.J. [Collection]. New York Public Library [The]. Image ID: 1606993.
- Unknown. 1859 Egyptian Artillerie Unteroffizier. Vinkhuijzen, H.J. [Collection]. New York Public Library [The]. Image ID: 1606988.
- Unknown. 1859 Egyptian Leibgarde 1. Escadron, Cario. Vinkhuijzen, H.J. [Collection]. New

- York Public Library [The]. Image ID: 1606997.
- Unknown. 1859 Egyptian Leibgarde 2. Escadron, Cario. Vinkhuijzen, H.J. [Collection]. New York Public Library [The]. Image ID: 1606996.
- Unknown. 1859 Egyptian Leibgarde 3. Escadron, Cario. Vinkhuijzen, H.J. [Collection]. New York Public Library [The]. Image ID: 1606995.
- Unknown. 1859 Egyptian Guard Hussar. Vinkhuijzen, H.J. [Collection]. New York Public Library [The]. Image ID: 1606999.
- Unknown. 1851 Egyptische Artillerie. Vinkhuijzen, H.J. [Collection]. New York Public Library [The]. Image ID: 1606985.
- Unknown. 1849 Turkisches Militar. Vinkhuijzen, H.J. [Collection]. New York Public Library [The]. Image ID: 418803.
- Unknown. 1841 Distinguishing Flags of the Egyptian and Ottoman Navy. Illustrated Table of Flags.
- Unknown. 1840 Egyptian Infantryman Leaning on Rifle. Picture. Anne S.K. Brown Military Collection: BDR 226199.
- Unknown. 1830 Zirkhli. Vinkhuijzen, H.J. [Collection]. New York Public Library [The]. Image ID: 1606998.
- Walsh, T. 1803 Journal of the Late Campaign in Egypt. Cadell & Davies, Strand: London.
- War Office [The]. 2008 [The] 1915 Notes on the Imperial Army: With a Short Vocabulary of Turkish Words and Phrases. N & M Press.
- Wilkinson-Latham, R. 1976 The Sudan Campaigns 1881–98. Osprey Publishing.
- Williams, F. 1857 England's Battles by Sea and Land: Russia and Turkey. Volume III. The London Printing and Publishing Company.
- Winter, M. 2003 Egyptian Society Under Ottoman Rule, 1517-1798. Routledge.
- Woodville, R.C. 1895 Egyptian Cavallerie. Drawing. Anne S.K. Brown Military Collection Item BDR: 312918.

OTHER TITLES BY THE SAME AUTHOR

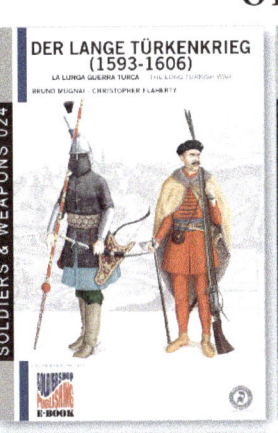

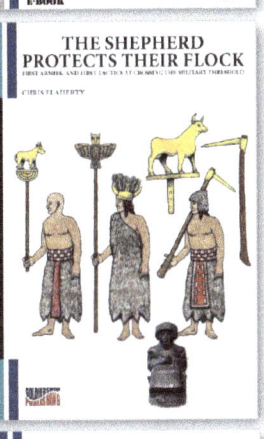

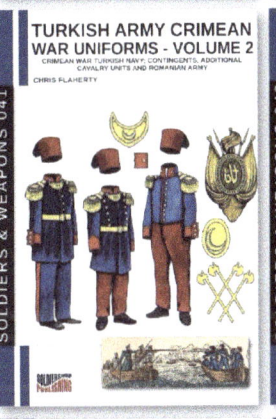

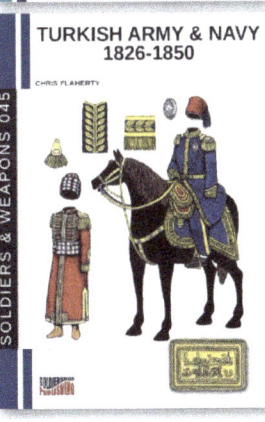
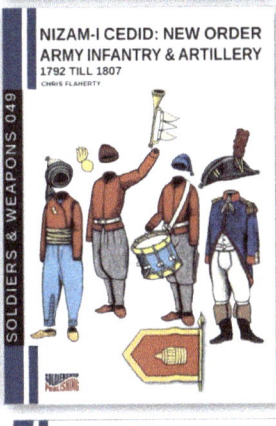
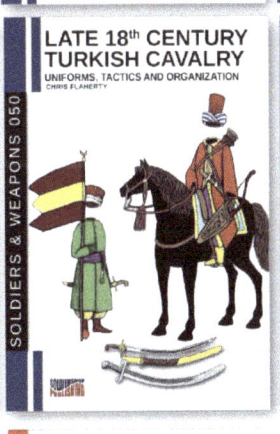
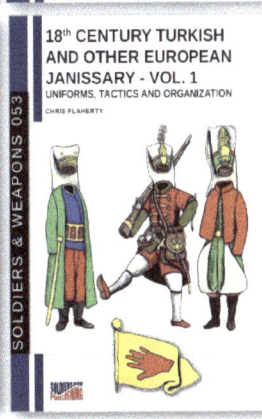
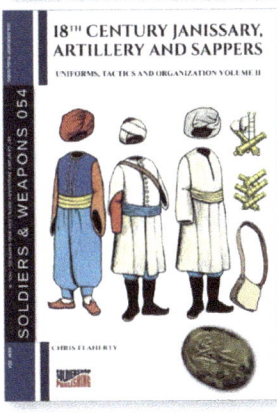
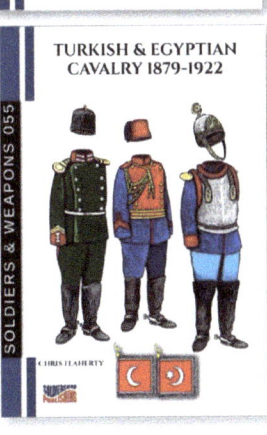
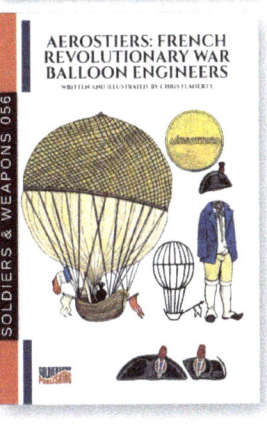
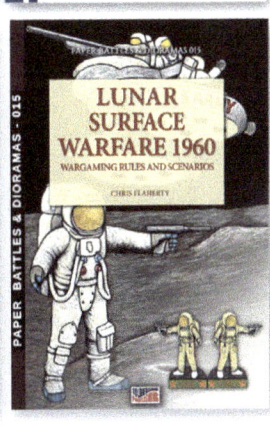

SOLDIERS & WEAPONS 057